10th Workshop on Challenges in the Management of Large Corpora (CMLC-10)

Held at LREC 2022

Marseille, France
20 – 25 June 2022

Editors:

Piotr Banski
Adrien Barbaresi
Simon Clematide
Marc Kupietz
Harald Lungen

ISBN: 978-1-7138-6115-7

Printed from e-media with permission by:

Curran Associates, Inc.
57 Morehouse Lane
Red Hook, NY 12571

CURRAN ASSOCIATES INC.
proceedings
.com

Some format issues inherent in the e-media version may also appear in this print version.

Association for Computational Linguistics
209 N. Eighth Street
Stroudsburg, Pennsylvania 18360

Phone: 1-570-476-8006
Fax: 1-570-476-0860

acl@aclweb.org

Additional copies of this publication are available from:

Curran Associates, Inc.
57 Morehouse Lane
Red Hook, NY 12571 USA
Phone: 845-758-0400
Fax: 845-758-2633
Email: curran@proceedings.com
Web: www.proceedings.com

LREC 2022 Workshop
Language Resources and Evaluation Conference
20-25 June 2022

Challenges in the Management of Large Corpora (CMLC-10)

PROCEEDINGS

Editors:
Piotr Bański, Adrien Barbaresi, Simon Clematide,
Marc Kupietz, Harald Lüngen

Proceedings of the LREC 2022 Workshop on Challenges in the Management of Large Corpora (CMLC-10 2022)

Edited by:
Piotr Bański, Adrien Barbaresi, Simon Clematide, Marc Kupietz, Harald Lüngen

For more information:
European Language Resources Association (ELRA)
9 rue des Cordelières
75013, Paris
France
http://www.elra.info
Email: lrec@elda.org

Preface

Creating very large corpora no longer appears to be a challenge. With the constantly growing amount of born-digital text – be it available on the web or only on the servers of publishing companies – and with the rising number of printed texts digitised by public institutions or technological giants such as Google, we may safely expect the upper limits of text collections to keep increasing for years to come. Although some of this was already true 20 years ago, we have a strong impression that the challenge has now shifted from an increase in terms of size to the effective and efficient processing of the large amounts of primary data and much larger amounts of annotation data.

On the one hand, some fundamental technical methods and strategies call for re-evaluation. These include, for example, efficient and sustainable curation of data, management of collections that span multiple volumes or that are distributed across several centres, innovative corpus architectures that maximise the usefulness of data, and techniques that allow for efficient search and analysis.

On the other hand, the new challenges require research into language-modelling methods and new corpus-linguistic methodologies that can make use of extremely large, semi-structured datasets. These methodologies must re-address the tasks of investigating rare phenomena involving multiple lexical items, of finding and representing fine-grained sub-regularities, and of investigating variations within and across language domains. This should be accompanied by new methods to structure both content and search results, in order to, among others, cope with false positives, assess data quality, or ensure interoperability. Another much-needed research goal is visualisation techniques that facilitate the interpretation of results and formulation of new hypotheses.

Due to the interest that the first meeting of CMLC (held at LREC-2012 in Istanbul) enjoyed, the workshop became a cyclic event. The second meeting took place at LREC again, in 2014 in Reykjavík; the third edition of CMLC was part of Corpus Linguistics 2015 in Lancaster. The fourth meeting took place in Portorož, Slovenia, as part of LREC-2016. CMLC-5 was an event combined with BigNLP-2017 and took place as part of the Corpus Linguistics conference in Birmingham. The sixth meeting took us to Japan (LREC-2018 in Miyazaki), and the seventh to Wales (CL 2019 in Cardiff). Due to the COVID-19 pandemic, the eighth event, scheduled to be co-located with LREC-2020 in Marseille, shared the fate of the conference and was cancelled at the post-review stage, while we chose to maintain the event numbering for the sake of the proceedings volume. The subsequent meeting, at CL 2021, organised by the University of Limerick, was fully virtual.

In 2022, as part of this year's LREC, we are going to meet in hybrid mode, the physical part of which is going to be Marseille. The leading questions for papers and discussions during CMLC-10 are: (a) What can be done to deal with IPR and data protection issues? (b) What sampling techniques can we apply? (c) What quality issues should we be aware of? (d) What infrastructures and frameworks are being developed for the efficient storage, annotation, analysis and retrieval of large datasets? (e) What affordances do visualisation techniques offer for the exploratory analysis approaches of corpora? (f) What kinds of APIs or other means of access would make the corpus data as widely usable as possible without interfering with legal restrictions? (g) How to guarantee that corpus data remain available and sustainably usable?

We would like to thank the Authors and the Programme Committee for their effort, and we are looking forward to meeting or seeing many of you in person, at last.

Piotr Bański, Adrien Barbaresi, Simon Clematide, Marc Kupietz, Harald Lüngen

Organizers

Piotr Bański – Leibniz-Institut für Deutsche Sprache, Mannheim
Adrien Barbaresi – Berlin-Brandenburg Academy of Sciences
Simon Clematide – University of Zurich
Marc Kupietz – Leibniz-Institut für Deutsche Sprache, Mannheim
Harald Lüngen – Leibniz-Institut für Deutsche Sprache, Mannheim

Program Committee:

Laurence Anthony, Waseda University (Japan)
Vladimír Benko, Slovak Academy of Sciences (Slovakia)
Damir Ćavar, Indiana University (USA)
Nils Diewald, IDS Mannheim (Germany)
Tomaž Erjavec, Jožef Stefan Institute, Ljubljana (Slovenia)
Johannes Graën, University of Zurich (Switzerland)
Andrew Hardie, Lancaster University (UK)
Serge Heiden, ENS de Lyon/IHRIM (France)
Miloš Jakubíček, Lexical Computing Ltd. (UK)
Paweł Kamocki, IDS Mannheim (Germany)
Natalia Kotsyba, Samsung (Poland)
Dawn Knight, Cardiff University (UK)
Michal Křen, Charles University, Prague (Czech Republic)
Veronika Laippala, University of Turku (Finland)
Verena Lyding, EURAC Research (Italy)
Paul Rayson, Lancaster University (UK)
Laurent Romary, INRIA (France)
Jan-Oliver Rüdiger, IDS Mannheim (Germany)
Roman Schneider, IDS Mannheim (Germany)
Serge Sharoff, University of Leeds (UK)
Irena Spasić, Cardiff University (UK)
Marko Tadić, University of Zagreb (Croatia)
Ludovic Tanguy, University of Toulouse (France)
Tamás Váradi, Hungarian Academy of Sciences (Hungary)
Andreas Witt, IDS / University of Mannheim (Germany)

Table of Contents

Workshop Program

Monday, June 20, 2022

09:00–10:30 Session 1

9:00–9:15 *Technical Setup and Welcome*

9:15–9:30 *Intro*

9:30–10:00 *Challenges in Creating a Representative Corpus of Romanian Micro-Blogging Text*
Vasile Pais, Maria Mitrofan, Verginica Barbu Mititelu, Elena Irimia, Roxana Micu and Carol Luca Gasan

10:00–10:30 *Exhaustive Indexing of PubMed Records with Medical Subject Headings*
Modest von Korff

10:00–11:00 Coffee Break

11:00–13:00 Session 2

11:00–11:30 *UDeasy: a Tool for Querying Treebanks in CoNLL-U Format*
Luca Brigada Villa

11:30–12:00 *Matrix and Double-Array Representations for Efficient Finite State Tokenization*
Nils Diewald

12:00–12:30 *Count-Based and Predictive Language Models for Exploring DeReKo*
Peter Fankhauser and Marc Kupietz

12:30–13:00 *"The word expired when that world awoke." New Challenges for Research with Large Text Corpora and Corpus-Based Discourse Studies in Totalitarian Times*
Hanno Biber

Challenges in Creating a Representative Corpus of Romanian Micro-Blogging Text

Vasile Păiș, Maria Mitrofan, Elena Irimia, Verginica Barbu Mititelu, Roxana Micu, Carol Luca Gasan
Research Institute for Artificial Intelligence "Mihai Drăgănescu", Romanian Academy
Bucharest, Romania
{vasile,maria,elena,vergi}@racai.ro

Abstract

Short text messages used in micro-blogging platforms have specific characteristics making them difficult to process with existing natural language tools, trained on regular text. This paper presents challenges encountered while creating a representative corpus of Romanian micro-blogging text; in this phase we focus on Twitter messages. Once completed, this would become an extension of the Representative Corpus of the Contemporary Romanian Language (CoRoLa) and will be made available to the research community using similar interfaces.

Keywords: large corpus, micro-blogging text, natural language processing, Romanian language

1. Introduction

Following the successful creation of a national representative corpus of the contemporary Romanian language (Tufiș et al., 2019), we turned our attention to the social media texts, as present in micro-blogging platforms. These platforms are characterized by brevity, thus the high number of contractions, abbreviations and emoticons to convey messages. They are also informal manifestation of communication, sometimes even colloquial. Using snippets of text in a foreign language is sometimes a way of making the message shorter and faster to deliver, but such strings also carry pragmatic information (Vogh, 2022). Code-switching can occur frequently in such messages, making them difficult to process and even to detect automatically the languages employed by the user (Das and Gambäck, 2013). Furthermore, specific features such as hashtags, user references and links are also present. All these characteristics of the language used in micro-blogging make models trained on regular texts to be less effective on micro-blogging texts. This has lead to the creation of specialized language models, such as the contextual model BERTweet (Nguyen et al., 2020) or the Spanish COVID-19 Twitter embeddings (Miranda-Escalada et al., 2021a; Miranda-Escalada et al., 2021b). By using such dedicated contextual models, it becomes possible to outperform other general models on downstream tasks applied to micro-blogging text. However, such dedicated models are not available for all languages, and more specifically they are not available for the Romanian language.

Twitter is one of the most popular micro-blogging platforms. In recent years it has been used for studying the propagation of different news, including COVID-19 information (Lopez and Gallemore, 2021; Larson, 2020). It offers a high-level API, allowing searching for tweets based on different criteria, including specific queries and language. We started the creation of a Romanian micro-blogging corpus by employing this API to gather a large collection of text[1]. However, in spite of the easiness to build the raw text collection, we are faced with different issues regarding corpus annotation and management. Even though additional platforms will be considered for inclusion in a later stage (such as Reddit, Tumblr or Gab), we consider that tackling the problems related to Twitter messages will be a relevant step for all the micro-blogging content. Hence, currently, we are focusing on the Twitter platform.

Our main goal is to make the micro-blogging corpus part of the representative corpus of the Romanian language, allowing it to be exploited in the same way. This means a similar processing pipeline must be applicable. Finally, the resulting data needs to be indexed consistently. The national corpus is indexed by the KorAP Corpus Analysis Platform (Bański et al., 2012) and is queried by users familiar with its query languages and web interface. For centralization purposes and for facilitating the user experience, it would make sense to use the same platform for the new micro-blogging corpus.

In this paper, we present the current activities as well as the challenges faced when trying to apply existing tools (for both annotation and indexing) to a Romanian language micro-blogging corpus. These challenges are encountered at all annotation levels, including tokenization, and at the indexing stage. We consider that existing tools for Romanian language processing must be adapted to recognize features such as emoticons, emojis, hashtags, unusual abbreviations, elongated words (commonly used for emphasis in micro-blogging), multiple words joined together (within or outside hashtags), and code-mixed text: see the adaptations to social media of processing tools such as Stan-

[1]The gathering process is still in progress

Proceedings of the CMLC-10 Workshop (@LREC 2022), pages 1–7
Marseille, 20 June 2022

ford part of speech tagger (Derczynski et al., 2013), OpenNLP (Ritter et al., 2011), or GATE (Bontcheva et al., 2013). We analyse these features with emphasis on the Romanian language.
The paper is organized as follows: Section 2 presents related work, Section 3 describes the corpus collection process, Section 4 provides challenges related to corpus indexing, Section 5 introduces a manually annotated sub-corpus, and finally conclusions are given in Section 6.

2. Related work

Among different types of corpora, a new one has emerged in the last decades: computer-mediated communication (CMC) corpus. It includes collections of blog posts, forums posts, comments on news websites, social media, mobile phone applications, e-mails and chat rooms exchanges. Corpora of texts from social media platforms of the type micro-blogging have been collected for various languages: German and Danish (Bick, 2020), English (Sharma et al., 2020), Turkish (Çöltekin, 2020), Chinese (Wang et al., 2012), Romanian (Manolescu and Çöltekin, 2021), Arabic (Zaatari et al., 2016), Italian (Sanguinetti et al., 2018), French (Mazoyer et al., 2020) and others[2]
The interest in working with texts collected from such sources manifest in connection to various tasks, such as sentiment analysis applications development (Sharma et al., 2020; Cieliebak et al., 2017), the need to improve NLP tasks such as word segmentation (Wang et al., 2012), annotation of emotions (Roberts et al., 2012), credibility analysis (Zaatari et al., 2016), event detection (Mazoyer et al., 2020), linguistic phenomena manifested on micro-blogging platforms (Coats, 2019) and others. However, detection of hate speech is the interest preoccupying most of those focusing their research on micro-blogging platforms (Bick, 2020; Çöltekin, 2020; Manolescu and Çöltekin, 2021; Sanguinetti et al., 2018).
Developers and maintainers of large, usually national corpora have manifested interest in reflecting the language from social media sites, including micro-blogging platforms, in their data (Kren, 2020).

3. Corpus collection

For the purposes of gathering the Twitter corpus, we constructed a crawler employing the Twitter API for Academic Research. Since we are interested both in Romanian-only tweets and in code-mixed texts (employing at least a few Romanian words), the crawler can use either the Twitter language detection or queries based on lists of expressions constructed by hand. The queries are periodically executed retrieving newly posted messages. Furthermore, even though it currently integrates only the Twitter API, the crawler is built in a modular way, allowing the use of other APIs in the future.

Listing 1: Example retweeted message

```
RT @AnonymousUser1: A long retweeted
message that gets trunc...
```

Messages are retrieved in the API specific JSON format. Following the retrieval, a second process transforms the messages into text documents. At this step a filtering operation is applied in order to remove duplicated messages (employing the message identifier) and to apply a primary anonymization function by removing usernames and URLs. We further remove messages that contain less than 3 words.
Specific to social networks is the sharing of messages with a user's friends or followers. In Twitter this mechanism is called retweeting. The same message is redistributed by another user with only small changes: possibly adding "RT" in front of the message, and sometimes adding the user that initially posted the message. In case of long messages the retweeted message could get truncated to obey the API size restrictions. An example of a possible retweet associated with the message "A long retweeted message that gets truncated." is given in Listing 1. It is worth noting that technically there is no rule about the way a retweeted message should look like. The actual format is dependent on the application used to generate the message. Some retweets do not start with "RT", do not contain a user being mentioned or even contain a list of users.
From a linguistic perspective, the presence of retweets does not provide any useful information. Truncation of messages further complicates their processing. Therefore, in the final version of the corpus, such messages will be removed to avoid unnecessary text duplication. Preliminary statistics on the collected data indicate a number of 759,719 raw JSON files. After applying the process of removing tweets with less than 3 words and converting to text, we are currently left with 741,940 text files. These files will need to undergo a final operation of removing retweets. The already removed files contain mostly user mentions, URLs, emojis or emoticons. However, a closer look at the removed files show the presence of messages such as "Felicitări, @AnonymousUser! <url>" ("Congratulations, @AnonymousUser! <url>"). Even though such messages may be deemed uninteresting, it is still debatable whether or not to keep a small number of files for indexing or for training language models.

4. Corpus indexing

Krill[3], the search module in KorAP, indexes and provides search opportunities on textual data (the Twitter content in our case), various layers of annotation data

[2] Some CMC corpora are available for browsing or download in a CLARIN repository at `https://www.clarin.eu/resource-families/cmc-corpora`.

[3] https://github.com/KorAP/Krill

and the documents metadata (Diewald and Margaretha, 2016). Micro-blogging posts have specific characteristics in terms of metadata, that are not in the lines of the metadata used to describe and index CoRoLa: for example, instead of an author (as documents in CoRoLa and other KorAP indexed corpora have), a tweet has a username associated to it. However, due to anonymization requirements, this username may not be used in a publicly available interface. Furthermore, to reduce de-anonymization attacks it is not feasible to replace a username with the same identifier in multiple instances. Document classification metadata fields usually used to index corpora may be difficult to provide: the domain for each post is not easy to identify, even if the corpus gathering process is based on a curated term list, while a literary genre specific to social media is yet to be theorised. A Twitter post has no title, publisher or other regular metadata fields. Nevertheless, other characteristics may be present, such as if the message is part of a conversation or if it is a retweet.

For indexing the corpus in KorAP Corpus Analysis Platform, a conversion chain has to be executed to convert the local data and metadata files first to the I5 format (Lüngen and Sperberg-McQueen, 2012) (which is a TEI customization used in the German Reference Corpus DeReKo (Kupietz et al., 2010)), then to a proprietary KorAP-XML [4] format and finally to a format compatible with the Krill indexer. At the moment, there is a simple solution to deal with the Twitter metadata that has already been used for Twitter-Sample Corpus in DeReKo: I5 metadata format was extended to support external links with arbitrary titles to reference the Twitter posts, since the title field is a mandatory field in KorAP indexing process. For dealing with metadata information about retweets, replies, hashtags and other Twitter specific metadata information, a special class could be written in the future in korapxml2krill[5]. The KorAP platform distributes data annotation on different layers, with a base layer containing the form of the word and subsequent layers dealing with e.g. lemma information, morpho-syntactic information (POS tagging), syntactic information, etc. The Twitter corpus comes with a supplementary layer for the specific named entity (NE) annotation, which will require further adaptations of the indexing process.

For releasing the corpus, we need to provide sufficient anonymization, as demanded by different regulations, such as the GDPR, and also comply with Twitter's requirements. We examine the suitability of existing anonymization solutions for the Romanian language (Păiș et al., 2021a), and find they also need to be made aware of micro-blogging specific features, such as user specification and people names appearing in hashtags or in other unusual formats (lowercase letters, elongated names, first name and last name joined together without spaces).

A micro-blogging corpus comes with the additional challenge of being composed of a large number of files. Each file contains only a small number of sentences (usually one sentence). This may impose additional restrictions on the storage sub-system, for both processing and querying, requiring the ability to handle such a large number of files. However, it also offers an opportunity to exploit parallel processing pipelines, where the text can be distributed across a large number of processes, hosted on multiple servers. Prior to indexing it, the corpus must be tokenized and enhanced with token-level annotations. For this purpose, the available parallelization features in our RELATE platform (Păiș et al., 2020) are exploited in order to process a large volume of text in a manageable amount of time.

5. Manually annotated sub-corpus

In order to properly evaluate existing Romanian text processing pipelines and potentially train new ones specific to micro-blogging text, a small sub-corpus will be manually annotated. In a first phase, this annotation process will include named entity identification and classification of code-mixed messages (identifying also messages mostly written in foreign languages). Named entities will be marked at text span level, thus enabling us to check existing tokenization tools. As previously mentioned, we expect to encounter issues with named entities embedded in hashtags or other specific text structures.

In order to annotate the corpus with named entities, nine classes of entities were chosen. These classes will allow for evaluating recently created Romanian language NER systems (Păiş et al., 2021; Păiș, 2019; Mitrofan and Păiş, 2022; Mitrofan, 2019) and will account for the social messaging activities in the context of the COVID-19 pandemic. Each class of entities is briefly described below:

- Organization (ORG) entities are limited to corporations, agencies, and other groups of people defined by an established organizational structure. The annotation process will mark text spans clearly indicating the name of an organization. Examples: *Facebook*, *Guvernul* ("*the government*"), *PSD*, *#ConsConRo*.

- Person (PER) entities are regularly limited to humans. A person may be a single individual or a group. By extension, the same label is attached to fictional characters or references to religious figures. Examples: *Adela*, *Moș Crăciun* ("*Santa Claus*"), *Niculina Stoican*.

- Location (LOC) entities are limited to geographical entities such as geographical areas and landmasses, bodies of water, and geological formations, denoted by a proper name. The annotation process will identify the name associated with a

[4] https://github.com/KorAP/KorAP-XML-Krill#about-korap-xml

[5] https://github.com/KorAP/KorAP-XML-Krill

location entity, without additional words, unless these words are part of the official entity name. Examples: *România*, *Parcul Tineretului*, *Lacul Sfânta Ana* ("*Lake Saint Ana*").

- Time (TIME) expressions tell us when something happened, how long something lasted, or how often something occurs. Sometimes the precise date cannot be determined, allowing for expressions indicating periods of time. Examples: *astăzi* ("*today*"), *15 septembrie* ("*September 15*"), *Crăciun* ("Christmas").

- Legal references (LEGAL) are designations (the title of a legal document) or expressions pointing to another legal document. Examples: *legea 13/2021* ("*law 13/2021*"), *constituția* ("*the Constitution*").

- Anatomical parts (ANAT) class contains mentions of anatomical parts, parts of the human body, organs, components of organs, tissues, cells, cellular components. Examples: *cap* ("*head*"), *mâini* ("*hands*"), *ficat* ("*liver*").

- Chemical and drugs (CHEM) class contains mentions of amino acids, peptides, proteins, antibiotics, active substances, drugs, enzymes, hormones, receptors. Examples: *sodiu* ("*sodium*"), *vaccin* ("*vaccine*").

- Disorders (DISO) class contains mentions of anatomical abnormalities, congenital anomalies, diseases, syndromes, lesions, symptoms. Examples: *diabet* ("*diabetes*"), *COVID*.

- Medical devices (MED_DEVICE) class contains mentions of any device intended to be used for medical purposes. Examples: *stetoscop* ("*stethoscope*").

The annotators followed specific guidelines, inspired in part by the Linguistic Data Consortium (LDC) guidelines [6] for annotation of named entities. More specifically, regarding the annotations with the ORG, PER, LOC and LEGAL classes, the guidelines presented in both previous works (Păiș, 2019; Păiş et al., 2021) were followed. In order to annotate the corpus with named entities specific to the medical domain (CHEM, DISO, MED_DEVICE), the annotators followed the specific guidelines described in (Mitrofan, 2017; Mitrofan et al., 2019). However, these guidelines had to be adapted to include elements specific to micro-blogging texts, such as NEs present in hashtags, unusual abbreviations or spelling, and words linked together.
Similar to other NE gold corpora creation activities, we had to clearly define each type of entity. During the annotation process some issues were identified and required further clarifications. Nevertheless, since we also wanted to be able to use the newly annotated corpus to evaluate and adapt existing tools to the social-media domain, we were constrained by already existing annotation guidelines, such as the one[7] used for annotating the LegalNERo corpus (Păiș et al., 2021b). Some interesting NE annotation instances that we encountered and needed to be deliberated were:

- metonymies of the type places for organizations are also annotated as LOC: in "Thailand will organize the voting process" the word "Thailand" is annotated as LOC, though it refers to the government of the country;

- imbricated entities are not annotated: only the wider string is annotated: e.g., in the string *primăria din Tecuci* one could identify two entities: the LOC *Tecuci* and the ORG *primăria din Tecuci*; however, only the latter is annotated. An exception is made for the LEGAL entity class which has sub-entities annotated (this is due to the LegalNERo guidelines);

- only sequences that unambiguously identify a named entity are annotated: e.g., *un frate al lui Mbape* "one of Mbape's brothers" may refer to any of Mbape's brothers, thus not being annotated, while *Mbape* is a clearly identified person. However "podul peste Dunăre de la Brăila" ("Brăila bridge over the Danube") is a location entity since it is clearly defined, even though it lacks an actual name.

Classification of the tweet files is done according to 4 different axes, which will be encoded in the corpus as attributes at metadata level:

- Language = *Romanian* or *Mixed RO+English* or *Mixed RO+Other* or *Other*. For this attribute, we based our classification on the distinction between linguistic borrowing and code-switching phenomena: the borrowing occurs at lexical level - mostly when the concept to be expressed is not lexicalised in the spoken language or when the speaker has a momentary lapse - and it involves using a single (simple or compound) word from another language; the code-switching occurs at the syntactic level - for pragmatic reasons like communicating emotions or the need to be understood only by some listeners and not others - and it involves the alternative use of (most often) two languages by combining longer sequences of words.

- Sentiment = *Neutral* or *Positive* or *Negative*. The Sentiment is Positive or Negative if it is directly

[6] https://www.ldc.upenn.edu/sites/www.ldc.upenn.edu/files/english-edt-v4.2.6.pdf

[7] https://relate.racai.ro/resources/legalnero/legalnero_annotation_guide.pdf

expressed by the tweet author but the text is classified as Neutral if it speaks in objective/journalistic manner about an unhappy event.

- Hate = *No* or *Yes*. This attribute encodes the presence in the tweet text of hate speech elements, expressed by harmful and offensive statements against specific categories of persons or even certain persons.
- Language Type = *Regular* or *Social Media Slang*. This attribute is meant to spot messages using micro-blogging specific language (the so-called social media slang), clearly different from regular text (for example "LOL!!! :) :D").

Both annotation and classification are handled within the RELATE[8] platform (Păiș et al., 2020; Păiș, 2020). For NER annotations, we defined a custom profile for the integrated BRAT[9] (Stenetorp et al., 2012) component. Classification is handled through a custom component available in the RELATE platform. The annotator's interface is shown in Figure 1.

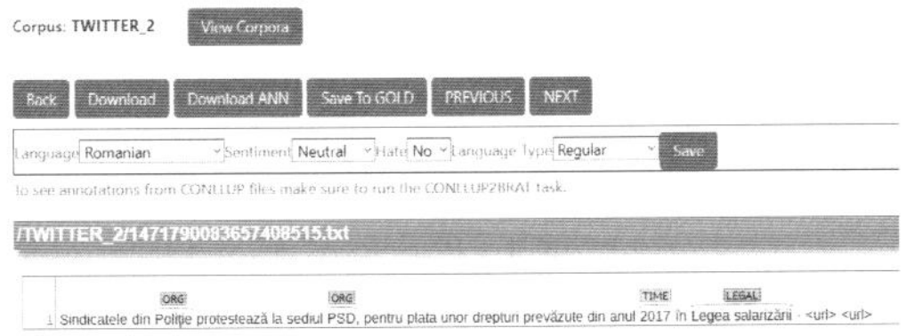

Figure 1: Annotation interface within the RELATE platform.

The tweets were split into multiple batches (with 500 messages in each batch) which were distributed amongst annotators (currently 7 annotators are involved). A number of files are common between at least three annotators, which will allow us to compute inter-annotator agreement metrics at the end of the annotation process. Periodic meetings are being held in order to identify and document potential issues early in the process, discuss and decide upon the right solutions. In order to encourage a certain level of competition between annotators, a simple dashboard was developed within the RELATE platform. This presents basic information, such as the number of files each annotator worked on and a graphical display (with changing colors) indicating the remaining work to be done. A snapshot of the dashboard is given in Figure 2.

The current annotation effort aims at annotating 21 batches of 500 messages. Each batch is split into 300 files unique to the batch and 200 files found in two other batches for agreement calculation. This leads to a number of 7,800 total distinct messages. Computing

[8]https://relate.racai.ro

[9]https://brat.nlplab.org/

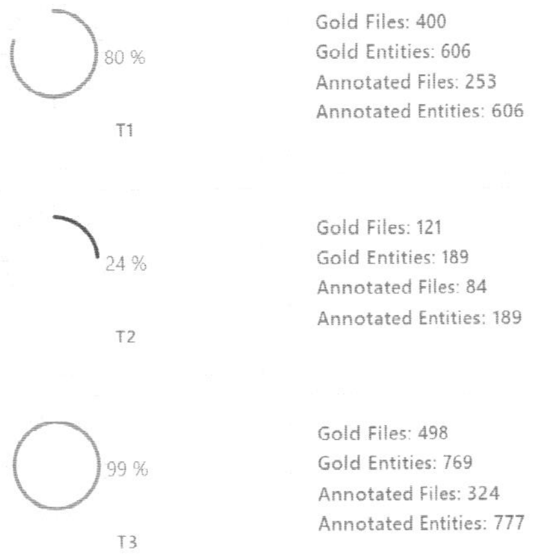

Figure 2: Dashboard for the annotation process.

the average number of entities annotated in 7 batches, we notice the presence of 733 NEs in each batch (corresponding to 1.47 NEs in each file). Therefore we estimate a final value of approximately 11,466 total entities.

6. Conclusion

This paper introduced the first steps taken towards extending the representative corpus of the contemporary Romanian language (CoRoLa) with a micro-blogging corpus. At this stage we focused only on Twitter, while developing the mechanisms which will allow us to extend the endeavour to other social media platforms as well. We presented the challenges encountered while working on this new Romanian corpus and we are actively working on solving the remaining issues. Furthermore, we are currently creating a manually annotated gold sub-corpus which will allow us to evaluate existing tools for micro-blogging text and train dedicated models. In turn, this will allow us to extend existing Romanian anonymization tools (Păiș et al., 2021a) to properly anonymize micro-blogging text.

We aim to make the final corpus available through the same indexing platform (KorAP) used for CoRoLa, thus enabling existing users to take advantage of the new resource in a similar way. Properly anonymized sub-corpora, such as the manually annotated gold corpus introduced in this paper, will also be made available for download in different formats, enabling other researchers to train and evaluate their own language models.

7. Bibliographical References

Bański, P., Fischer, P. M., Frick, E., Ketzan, E., Kupietz, M., Schnober, C., Schonefeld, O., and Witt, A. (2012). The new IDS corpus analysis platform:

Challenges and prospects. In *Proceedings of the Eighth International Conference on Language Resources and Evaluation (LREC'12)*, pages 2905–2911, Istanbul, Turkey, May. European Language Resources Association (ELRA).

Bick, E. (2020). An annotated social media corpus for German. In *Proceedings of the 12th Language Resources and Evaluation Conference*, pages 6127–6135, Marseille, France, May. European Language Resources Association.

Bontcheva, K., Derczynski, L., Funk, A., Greenwood, M. A., Maynard, D., and Aswani, N. (2013). Twitie: An open-source information extraction pipeline for microblog text. In *Proceedings of Recent Advances in Natural Language Processing*, pages 83–90, Hissar, Bulgaria.

Cieliebak, M., Deriu, J. M., Egger, D., and Uzdilli, F. (2017). A Twitter corpus and benchmark resources for German sentiment analysis. In *Proceedings of the Fifth International Workshop on Natural Language Processing for Social Media*, pages 45–51, Valencia, Spain, April. Association for Computational Linguistics.

Coats, S. (2019). Lexicon geupdated: New German anglicisms in a social media corpus. *European Journal of Applied Linguistics*, 7(2):255–280.

Çöltekin, Ç. (2020). A corpus of Turkish offensive language on social media. In *Proceedings of the 12th Language Resources and Evaluation Conference*, pages 6174–6184, Marseille, France, May. European Language Resources Association.

Das, A. and Gambäck, B. (2013). Code-mixing in social media text. the last language identification frontier? *Trait. Autom. des Langues*, 54:41–64.

Derczynski, L., Ritter, A., Clark, S., and Bontcheva, K. (2013). Twitter part-of-speech tagging for all: Overcoming sparse and noisy data. In *Proceedings of Recent Advances in Natural Language Processing*, page 198–206, Hissar, Bulgaria.

Diewald, N. and Margaretha, E. (2016). Krill: Korap search and analysis engine. *Journal for language technology and computational linguistics (JLCL)*, 31(1):73–90.

Kren, M. (2020). Czech national corpus in 2020: Recent developments and future outlook. In *Proceedings of the 8th Workshop on Challenges in the Management of Large Corpora*, pages 52–57, Marseille, France, May. European Language Ressources Association.

Kupietz, M., Belica, C., Keibel, H., and Witt, A. (2010). The German reference corpus DeReKo: A primordial sample for linguistic research. In *Proceedings of the Seventh International Conference on Language Resources and Evaluation (LREC'10)*.

Larson, H. J. (2020). A call to arms: helping family, friends and communities navigate the covid-19 infodemic. *Nature Reviews Immunology*, 20(8):449–450, Aug.

Lopez, C. E. and Gallemore, C. (2021). An augmented multilingual Twitter dataset for studying the COVID-19 infodemic. *Social Network Analysis and Mining*, 11(1):102, Oct.

Lüngen, H. and Sperberg-McQueen, C. M. (2012). A TEI P5 document grammar for the IDS text model. *Journal of the Text Encoding Initiative*, (3).

Manolescu, M. and Çöltekin, Ç. (2021). ROFF - a Romanian Twitter dataset for offensive language. In *Proceedings of the International Conference on Recent Advances in Natural Language Processing (RANLP 2021)*, pages 895–900, Held Online, September. INCOMA Ltd.

Mazoyer, B., Cagé, J., Hervé, N., and Hudelot, C. (2020). A French corpus for event detection on Twitter. In *Proceedings of the 12th Language Resources and Evaluation Conference*, pages 6220–6227, Marseille, France, May. European Language Resources Association.

Miranda-Escalada, A., Aguero, M., and Krallinger, M. (2021a). Spanish COVID-19 Twitter embeddings in FastText, January. Funded by the Plan de Impulso de las Tecnologías del Lenguaje (Plan TL).

Miranda-Escalada, A., Farré-Maduell, E., Lima-López, S., Gascó, L., Briva-Iglesias, V., Agüero-Torales, M., and Krallinger, M. (2021b). The ProfNER shared task on automatic recognition of occupation mentions in social media: systems, evaluation, guidelines, embeddings and corpora. In *Proceedings of the Sixth Social Media Mining for Health (# SMM4H) Workshop and Shared Task*, pages 13–20.

Mitrofan, M. and Păiş, V. (2022). Improving Romanian BioNER using a biologically inspired system. In *Proceedings of the 21st BioNLP workshop (paper accepted)*. Association for Computational Linguistics.

Mitrofan, M., Mititelu, V. B., and Mitrofan, G. (2019). Monero: a biomedical gold standard corpus for the romanian language. In *Proceedings of the 18th BioNLP Workshop and Shared Task*, pages 71–79.

Mitrofan, M. (2017). Bootstrapping a Romanian corpus for medical named entity recognition. In *RANLP*, pages 501–509.

Mitrofan, M. (2019). *Extragere de cunoștințe din texte în limba română și date structurate cu aplicații în domeniul medical*. Ph.D. thesis, Romanian Academy.

Nguyen, D. Q., Vu, T., and Tuan Nguyen, A. (2020). BERTweet: A pre-trained language model for English tweets. In *Proceedings of the 2020 Conference on Empirical Methods in Natural Language Processing: System Demonstrations*, pages 9–14, Online, October. Association for Computational Linguistics.

Păiş, V., Mitrofan, M., Gasan, C. L., Coneschi, V., and Ianov, A. (2021). Named entity recognition in the Romanian legal domain. In *Proceedings of the Natural Legal Language Processing Workshop 2021*, pages 9–18, Punta Cana, Dominican Republic, November. Association for Computational Linguistics.

Păiș, V., Ion, R., and Tufiș, D. (2020). A processing platform relating data and tools for Romanian language. In *Proceedings of the 1st International Workshop on Language Technology Platforms*, pages 81–88, Marseille, France. European Language Resources Association.

Păiș, V., Irimia, E., Ion, R., Tufiș, D., Mitrofan, M., Barbu Mititelu, V., Avram, A.-M., and Curea, E. (2021a). Romanian text anonymization experiments from the CURLICAT project. In *The 16th International Conference on Linguistic Resources and Tools for Natural Language Processing*, pages 165–178.

Păiș, V., Mitrofan, M., Gasan, C. L., Ianov, A., Ghiță, C., Coneschi, V. S., and Onuț, A. (2021b). Romanian Named Entity Recognition in the Legal domain (LegalNERo), May.

Păiș, V. (2019). *Contributions to semantic processing of texts; Identification of entities and relations between textual units; Case study on Romanian language*. Ph.D. thesis, School of Advanced Studies of the Romanian Academy (SCOSAAR), Bucharest, Romania, November.

Păiș, V. (2020). Multiple annotation pipelines inside the RELATE platform. In *The 15th International Conference on Linguistic Resources and Tools for Natural Language Processing*, pages 65–75.

Ritter, A., Clark, S., and Etzioni, O. (2011). Named entity recognition in tweets: An experimental study. In *Proceedings of the 2011 Conference on Empirical Methods in Natural Language Processing*, pages 1524–1534, Edinburgh, Scotland, UK.

Roberts, K., Roach, M. A., Johnson, J., Guthrie, J., and Harabagiu, S. M. (2012). EmpaTweet: Annotating and detecting emotions on Twitter. In *Proceedings of the Eighth International Conference on Language Resources and Evaluation (LREC'12)*, pages 3806–3813, Istanbul, Turkey, May. European Language Resources Association (ELRA).

Sanguinetti, M., Poletto, F., Bosco, C., Patti, V., and Stranisci, M. (2018). An Italian Twitter corpus of hate speech against immigrants. In *Proceedings of the Eleventh International Conference on Language Resources and Evaluation (LREC 2018)*, Miyazaki, Japan, May. European Language Resources Association (ELRA).

Sharma, R., Verma, A., Grover, R., Pandey, D., Pandey, B., and A, L. (2020). Microbloging as a corpus for sentiment analysis structure and feeling mining. *Journal of Xi'an Shiyou University, Natural Science Edition*, pages 229–234, 11.

Stenetorp, P., Pyysalo, S., Topić, G., Ohta, T., Ananiadou, S., and Tsujii, J. (2012). brat: a web-based tool for NLP-assisted text annotation. In *Proceedings of the Demonstrations at the 13th Conference of the European Chapter of the Association for Computational Linguistics*, pages 102–107, Avignon, France, April. Association for Computational Linguistics.

Tufiș, D., Barbu Mititelu, V., Irimia, E., Păiș, V., Ion, R., Diewald, N., Mitrofan, M., and Mihaela, O. (2019). Little strokes fell great oaks. creating CoRoLa, the reference corpus of contemporary romanian. *Revue Roumaine de Linguistique*, 64(3):227–240.

Vogh, K. (2022). Code-mixing and semantico-pragmatic. In *Points of Convergence in Romance Linguistics: Papers selected from the 48th Linguistic Symposium on Romance Languages (LSRL 48), Toronto, 25-28 April 2018*, volume 360, page 243. John Benjamins Publishing Company.

Wang, L., Wong, D. F., Chao, L. S., and Xing, J. (2012). CRFs-based Chinese word segmentation for micro-blog with small-scale data. In *Proceedings of the Second CIPS-SIGHAN Joint Conference on Chinese Language Processing*, pages 51–57, Tianjin, China, December. Association for Computational Linguistics.

Zaatari, A. A., Ballouli, R. E., ELbassouni, S., El-Hajj, W., Hajj, H., Shaban, K., Habash, N., and Yahya, E. (2016). Arabic corpora for credibility analysis. In *Proceedings of the Tenth International Conference on Language Resources and Evaluation (LREC'16)*, pages 4396–4401, Portorož, Slovenia, May. European Language Resources Association (ELRA).

Exhaustive Indexing of PubMed Records with Medical Subject Headings

Modest von Korff
Idorsia Pharmaceuticals Ltd.
Hegenheimermattweg 91, 4123 Allschwil, Switzerland
modest.korff@idorsia.com

Abstract

With fourteen million publication records the PubMed database is one of the largest repositories in medical science. Analyzing this database to relate biological targets to diseases is an important task in pharmaceutical research. We developed a software tool, MeSHTreeIndexer, for indexing the PubMed medical literature with disease terms. The disease terms were taken from the Medical Subject Heading (MeSH) Terms compiled by the National Institutes of Health (NIH) of the US. In a first semi-automatic step we identified about 5'900 terms as disease related. The MeSH terms contain so-called entry points that are synonymously used for the terms. We created an inverted index for these 5'900 MeSH terms and their 58'000 entry points. From the PubMed database fourteen million publication records were stored in Lucene. These publication records were tagged by the inverted MeSH term index. In this contribution we demonstrate that our approach provided a significant higher enrichment in MeSH terms than the indexing of the PubMed records by the NIH themselves. Manual control proved that our enrichment is meaningful.

Keywords: Text mining, MeSH, PubMed, Indexing

1. Introduction

The starting point for drug discovery is to find a new biological target to cure a disease. As always in drug discovery, first step is analysing the related medical literature. Therefore, searching the medical literature for diseases is a common task. Searching the life science literature for diseases belongs in the category of biomedical named entity recognition. With the increasing amount of information the interest in indexing biomedical information becomes of more and more interest. The largest repository for medical literature is provided by the National Institutes of Health (NIH) of the US (NIH, 2022b). In January 2022 the PubMed database contained 33 million records for biomedical literature compiled from MEDLINE, life science journals, and online books. For searching and indexing the medical records in PubMed the NIH developed a thesaurus, the Medical Subject Headings (NIH, 2022; Lipscomb, 2000). These MeSH terms are organized in a tree with 16 main branches. Branch A contains terms from anatomy, branch B lists organisms, branch C is dedicated to diseases, branch D lists chemicals and drugs, branch E structures analytical diagnostic and therapeutic techniques, and branch F organizes terms from psychiatry and psychology. The following branches contain terms from phenomena and processes (G), disciplines and occupations (H), anthropology (I), technology (J), humanities (K), information science (L), named groups (M), health care (N), publication characteristics (V), and geographicals (Z). For medical literature other indexing systems exist as well. Widely used is SNOMED, a collection of clinical terminology to represent patient data for clinical purposes (Ruch et al., 2008). Health insurances use a disease classification system 'International Classification of Diseases (ICD)', version 11 (World Health Organization, 2016). However, neither SNOMED nor ICD were intended to capture content of scientific literature. The MeSH terms were derived from the scientific literature in life sciences. The NIH index semi-automatically the PUBMED records with MeSH terms. Manual annotation processes are labour-intensive. It is a fact that the indexing is delayed and incomplete because of the amount of publications in life sciences and limited resources (Hadfield, 2020; Irwin and Rackham, 2017).

2. Related work

Because of the high importance for research in life science, automatic indexing systems for MeSH terms were developed. They can be classified into three categories: 1) pattern matching, 2) text classification, 3) learning-to-rank. From all software tools to be named, MetaMap (Aronson and Lang, 2010) was developed first by the US National Library of Medicine. MetaMap applies pattern matching to the unified medical language system UMLS. UMLS are not MeSH terms, but closely related. Indexing MeSH terms is PubTator, a web based indexing system also developed by the US National Library of Medicine (Wei et al., 2013). PubTator uses DNorm (Leaman et al., 2013) to tag PubMed articles with MeSH disease terms. DNorm is based on a pairwise learning-to-rank algorithm. Learning-to-rank algorithms make use of identified nearest neighbour documents to retrieve the most relevant MeSH terms (Huang et al., 2011). A more recent approach combines several machine learning techniques (Mao and Lu, 2017). Convolutional neural networks are used in (Gargiulo et al., 2019; Dai et al., 2020). MeSHLabeler uses a combination of Medical Text Indexer, pattern matching, and indexing rules (Liu

Proceedings of the CMLC-10 Workshop (@LREC 2022), pages 8–15
Marseille, 20 June 2022

et al., 2015). For all MeSH indexing must be considered that it is a complex task. Even between human indexers only 48.2% consistency was reported for main heading assignment (Funk and Reid, 1983). This unsatisfying consistency is easily explained by the aim of the indexing approaches. All here mentioned approaches aimed to index the literature with the most important concepts. But what are the most important concepts? This is often hard to recognize from the publication alone. Because, after a manuscript was published the relevance of its content depends on the context of the reader. The same publication has different meanings for two scientists studying different subjects.

3. Our work

Our goal was to index exhaustively a corpus of 14 million PubMed records with disease related MeSH terms. In contrary to all other approaches mentioned in the section above, we aimed to index every occurrence of a term. The major concept of a publication did not matter for us. The indexed corpus was intended to be analyzed for co-occurrences of index tags. A ranking of concepts was not intended. For this reason we decided to use a non-machine-learning approach for indexing. After analyzing the structure of the MeSH tree we realized that the information in the MeSH tree together with the entry terms would be sufficient for our needs. A node in the MeSH tree is labeled by a descriptor, e.g. diabetes mellitus, type 1. Additionally, so-called entry terms are given. These terms are synonyms, alternate forms, and other closely related terms that are generally used interchangeably with the descriptor term. For diabetes mellitus, type 1, 27 entry terms are given. These are terms which are alternatively used in life science literature. The alternative terms may differ only in a hyphen, order of words, complete different synonyms, or they are abbreviations. On average there are about ten entry points for each disease MeSH term. These entry points, in the following named as entry terms, represent the major forms of writing for a disease term in the life science literature. Our idea was to search for these entry points in the corpus of 14 million PubMed records. In the following section it is shown how we overcame many of the issues for text matching in medical literature, as it was discussed by Díaz and López in (Díaz and López, 2015).

4. Methods

4.1. Medical Subject Headings

For drug discovery purposes of interest are disease related terms. As described above, the MeSH tree contains 16 main branches. Two of these branches were used for disease indexing. The disease branch C and branch F, with terms from psychiatry and psychology. From these two branches unspecific expressions were removed. This included terms used as common words. These excluded expressions form a so-called stoplists. Stoplists for indexing disease MeSH terms were introduced by (Swanson et al., 2006). We loosely orientated our disease term collection at Swanson's stoplist. Very general disease terms were removed. Mainly entries from the psychology branch were removed, terms like affect, behavior, and aptitude. Additionally we took a list of the most common English words (Kaufman, 2017) to further exclude disease terms that are frequently used. Although, some common words are also important disease terms. So, a whitelist with needed disease terms was created. This whitelist contains disease terms like arthritis, measles and cholera. MeSH nodes are not unique in the MeSH tree. Because of the structure of the tree the same node can occur at more than one position. For example 'Gaucher Disease' is in branch 'Central Nervous System Diseases', 'Genetic Diseases, Inborn', 'Metabolic Diseases', and in other branches. The number of non-unique MeSH nodes sum up to 13'969. Finally, the disease MeSH tree contains 5'904 unique disease-related nodes. These nodes contain 63'072 entry points. In Table 1 a histogram is shown that represents the distribution of the entry points on the unique MeSH nodes.

Min bin	1	5	10	20	50
Max bin	5	10	20	50	1000
Counts	2161	1520	1357	771	94

Table 1: Histogram of the number of entry points in the disease MeSH terms

The MeSH terms and the entry terms were normalized for indexing. It is important to notice for our algorithm that the MeSH entry phrases contain the original terms in different orders, as they occur in the publications. Also alternatives with different punctuation marks, spelling variants and acronyms are given as entry terms. The 32 entry terms for the MeSH descriptor 'Diabetes Mellitus, Type 2' are given as example. The normalization procedure is described below in more detail for the PubMed records.

- Adult-Onset Diabetes Mellitus
- Diabetes Mellitus, Adult Onset
- Diabetes Mellitus, Adult-Onset
- Diabetes Mellitus, Ketosis Resistant
- Diabetes Mellitus, Ketosis-Resistant
- Diabetes Mellitus, Maturity Onset
- Diabetes Mellitus, Maturity-Onset
- Diabetes Mellitus, Non Insulin Dependent
- Diabetes Mellitus, Non-Insulin-Dependent
- Diabetes Mellitus, Noninsulin Dependent
- Diabetes Mellitus, Noninsulin-Dependent
- Diabetes Mellitus, Slow Onset
- Diabetes Mellitus, Slow-Onset
- Diabetes Mellitus, Stable

- Diabetes Mellitus, Type 2
- Diabetes Mellitus, Type II
- Diabetes, Maturity-Onset
- Diabetes, Type 2
- Ketosis-Resistant Diabetes Mellitus
- MODY
- Maturity Onset Diabetes
- Maturity Onset Diabetes Mellitus
- Maturity-Onset Diabetes
- Maturity-Onset Diabetes Mellitus
- NIDDM
- Non-Insulin-Dependent Diabetes Mellitus
- Noninsulin Dependent Diabetes Mellitus
- Noninsulin-Dependent Diabetes Mellitus
- Slow-Onset Diabetes Mellitus
- Stable Diabetes Mellitus
- Type 2 Diabetes
- Type 2 Diabetes Mellitus

These entry terms are text phrases frequently occurring in medical literature. After being normalized and stemmed, the number of terms reduced to 23.

- adult onset diabetes mellitus
- diabetes maturity onset
- diabetes mellitus adult onset
- diabetes mellitus ketosis resistant
- diabetes mellitus maturity onset
- diabetes mellitus non insulin dependent
- diabetes mellitus noninsulin dependent
- diabetes mellitus slow onset
- diabetes mellitus stable
- diabetes mellitus type 2
- diabetes mellitus type ii
- diabetes type 2
- ketosis resistant diabetes mellitus
- maturity onset diabetes
- maturity onset diabetes mellitus
- mody
- niddm
- non insulin dependent diabetes mellitus
- noninsulin dependent diabetes mellitus
- slow onset diabetes mellitus
- stable diabetes mellitus
- type 2 diabetes
- type 2 diabetes mellitus

To index a publication with the MeSH descriptor 'Diabetes Mellitus, Type 2' one of the 23 entry terms must be found in the text record. Therefore, the MeSH entry terms overcome many of the problems that were described by Díaz and López in (Díaz and López, 2015).

4.2. The MeSH term index tree

Apache Lucene was used to store the PubMed records, MeSH terms and the entry terms. Lucene is a widely used open-source database and text search engine (Białecki et al., 2012). Already, many string matching algorithms exist to search text indices. The best performing algorithms rely on preprocessing of a dictionary. So, a powerful key-word matching algorithm was developed by Aho and Corasick (Aho and Corasick, 1975). Their algorithm constructs a finite state pattern matching machine from the keywords. The keywords are processed once and the text is matched against the processed keywords. Another dictionary oriented approach used a modified Levenshtein distance for high-throughput spelling correction (Schulz and Mihov, 2002). Lucene contained the MeSH term index and is capable of text matching. So, in our first approach we tested the fuzzy search for multiple word terms in Lucene for indexing. Indexing performance was a major criteria for our algorithm. However, the indexing performance of Lucene was too low for the corpus of 14 million text records. It was also difficult to fine tune the fuzzy string matching. The matching criteria tended either be too coarse or too fine for a successful comparison. This was due to the structure of the MeSH terms, containing abbreviations and numbers. After several days of proprietary experiments with Lucene we decided to implement our own algorithm for performance reasons, and for better control of the matching terms. Our approach is similar to (Aho and Corasick, 1975), we also decided to implement a pre-processed tree-structure. With the difference, that the design of our algorithm was much simpler. It was tailored for our purpose to match medical subject headings. Medical subject headings are standardized phrases used in medical literature. They are collected in the MeSH terms and the entry terms. To prevent mismatches, matching a term needs to be exact. Only small typos or spelling variants may be accepted for a match. MeSH terms have significant meaning in medical literature. Typos at the beginning of a MeSH term phrase are not common. For this reason we decided that typos in the first character of a MeSH term result in a no-match. From the normalized entry terms a tree-based index was created and implemented as a list of lists. The first level of the tree represents the starting character of the normalized entry term. Numbers from 1 to 9 and lowercase letters a-z occur. The second list represents the number of tokens in the normalized entry term. As for the starting letter the number of tokens needs an exact match. A third list indexes the string length of the entry term. In the last list, the leaf node in the MeSH term index tree, the categorized normalized terms, are stored. As example: The MeSH descriptor 'Diabetes Mellitus, Type 2' contains the entry term 'Diabetes Mellitus, Non Insulin Dependent'. After being normalized the entry term becomes 'diabetes mellitus non insulin dependent'. First character of the normalized term is 'd', which equals index 39 in tree level one. The normalized entry term contains five tokens, index five in the second layer of the index tree. Finally, a length of 39 characters for the normalized entry term results in index 39 in tree level three. This node has three children: 'diabetes mellitus non insulin dependent', 'deficiencies fructose 1 6 diphosphatase', and 'diabetes insipidus nephrogenic x linked'. The normalized expressions occur without punctuation, hyphens and always in lowercase letters 1.

Figure 1: Part of the MeSH term index tree. Level one: starting letter of the MeSH term, level two: number of tokens, level three: number of characters, level four: MeSH term.

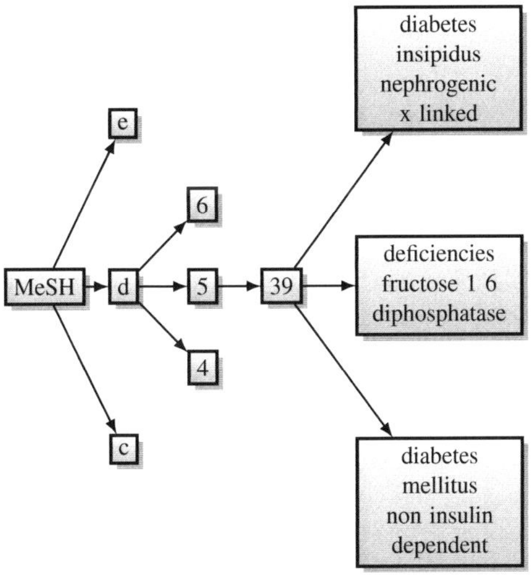

4.3. Searching for MeSH terms in PubMed records

PubMed records contain a lot of information, but they do not contain the full publication text. Publication title, abstract, and the PubMed identifier (PMID) were used for our algorithm. An example is given in Figure 2.

Searching a PubMed record for normalized MeSH terms starts by splitting the text into sentences, Figure 3. Searching is followed by stemming with the Apache OpenNLP library. The pre-processed phrases are tokenized. Every non-literal, Greek letters, written out Greek letters, and numbers directly attached to words are tokenized. Uppercase letters are converted into lowercase. Except, an uppercase letter is followed by another uppercase or by a number. There is no extra treatment for floating point numbers. Stop words are removed.

Publication title and abstract were used for MeSH term matching. Every phrase is parsed by the MeSH term index tree. Parsing is done phrase-wise with a sliding window of increasing size for the tokens in the phrase. Parsing starts with the first character of the first token

Figure 2: PubMed record for PMID 21965846. Part of the record, used for indexing. The typo in the title 'diabetis' instead of 'diabetes' is from the original publication.

A clinical evaluation of skin tags in relation to obesity, type 2 diabetis mellitus, age, and sex

Skin tags (STs) have been investigated as a marker of type 2 diabetes mellitus (DM), yet the relation of STs to obesity is still a matter of controversy. The aim of the study is to explore the relation of number, size and color of STs to obesity, diabetes, sex and age in one study. The study included 245 nondiabetic (123 males and 122 females) and 276 diabetic (122 males and 154 females) subjects. We recorded age, sex, body mass index (BMI), relevant habits, STs color, size, and number in different anatomical sites. The presence and the mean number of STs was more in obese than nonobese participants ($P = 0.006$ and $P < 0.001$, respectively) and was not affected by sex. However, the number increased significantly with age. The presence of mixed-color STs was related to obese ($P < 0.001$) participants. Multivariate logistic regression revealed that only BMI was significantly associated with the mixed-color STs ($OR = 3.5$, $P < 0.001$). The association of DM ($OR = 1.7$) with mixed-color STs was nonsignificant ($P = 0.073$). Neither age nor sex had any association with mixed-color STs. Within cases that developed mixed-color STs, the multivariate analysis showed that only BMI had a significant correlation to the number of STs (beta = 0.256, $P = 0.034$). The study showed that not only the number but also the presence of mixed-color ST was related to obesity, but not to diabetes. The presence of mixed-color STs in nondiabetic subjects needs close inspection of BMI. Keywords: Age; diabetes mellitus; obesity; sex; skin tags.

in the sentence. The node in level one that corresponds to the first character is the starting point for further parsing. Level two of the index tree corresponds to the number of tokens in the phrase. The number of tokens for the start phrase is 1. Level three of the index node corresponds to the number of characters in the phrase to analyze. All terms in the level three index nodes from minus three characters up to plus three characters are compared with the phrase to analyze. The comparison is a two step process. A first string match checks for misleading similarities. Misleading similarities are calculated from word pairs that differ by one or two characters but have a complete different meaning, e.g. injection and infection. If the word

Figure 3: Normalized and stemmed PubMed record for PMID 21965846. A period indicates the end of a phrase detected by the stemming algorithm.

> clinical evaluation skin tags relation obesity type 2 diabetis mellitus age sex. skin tags STs investigated marker type 2 diabetes mellitus DM relation STs obesity matter controversy. aim study explore relation number size color STs obesity diabetes sex age study. study included 245 nondiabetic 123 males 122 females 276 diabetic 122 males 154 females subjects. recorded age sex body mass index BMI relevant habits STs color size number different anatomical sites. presence mean number STs obese nonobese participants P 0 006 P 0 001 respectively affected sex. number increased significantly age. presence mixed color STs related obese P 0 001 participants. multivariate logistic regression revealed BMI significantly associated mixed color STs OR 3 5 P 0 001. association DM OR 1 7 mixed color STs nonsignificant P 0 073. age sex association mixed color STs. cases developed mixed color STs multivariate analysis showed BMI significant correlation number STs beta 0 256 P 0 034. study showed number presence mixed color ST related obesity diabetes. presence mixed color STs nondiabetic subjects needs close inspection BMI. keywords age diabetes mellitus obesity sex skin tags.

pair passes this test the similarity is calculated by the Damerau-Levenshtein algorithm. For phrase comparison with more than one token the comparison is done token by token. If the token pair similarity is below 0.75 the phrase is dissimilar. This threshold allows a small change in a word, i.e. the change of a single letter. This takes into account the morphological or orthographic variations of scientific writing. If the comparison matches the threshold, the average from all token pair comparisons in the phrase are calculated. If the average similarity is equal or above 0.85 the PubMed record is tagged with the MeSH descriptor corresponding to the matching phrase. MeSH entry terms are not necessarily unique, one matching phrase may result in two tags. An example is given with the string "Background: Skin tags (STs) have been investigated as a marker of type 2 diabetes mellitus (DM), yet the relation of STs to obesity is still a matter of controversy", PMID 21965846. The string is parsed after normalization. The following items demonstrate how the string is parsed with the sliding token window.

- 'background' → no match
- 'background skin' → no match
- 'background skin sts' → no match
- ...proceed up to maximum term length
- 'skin' → no match
- 'skin sts' → no match
- ...
- 'type' → no match
- 'type 2' → no match
- 'type 2 diabetes mellitus' → match
- 'diabetes' → no match
- 'diabetes mellitus' → match

The sentence is tagged with two MeSH descriptors 'Diabetes Mellitus' and 'Diabetes Mellitus, Type 2'. With this procedure all 14 million PubMed records were indexed with the matching MeSH term descriptors.

4.4. Implementation

The PubMed records were retrieved from the MEDLINE database and stored in Lucene (Białecki et al., 2012). The normalized PubMed records were also stored in Lucene. The MeSH term indexer was implemented in Java 11. The NIH MeSH tree was taken from the file mtrees2022.bin (NIH, 2022a). This file was serialized and stored. Entry terms were read on the fly from desc2022.xml. The disease MeSH tree was compiled from the serialized MeSH tree file, the descriptor file and the hard-coded stoplists. Index tags were written to the normalized records in Lucene.

5. Results

5.1. Results MeSH term index

A detailed view into the structure of the MeSH term index tree is given in the following section. As mentioned above, level one of the MeSH term index tree corresponds to the starting characters of the MeSH entry terms. In total, 58'774 unique MeSH entry terms were indexed in the MeSH term index tree. In Table 2 the counts for every starting character for all unique MeSH entry terms are shown. Some MeSH entry terms start with a number between 1 and 9, but none starts with a zero. The other characters are well distributed over the alphabet.

Char	Counts	Char	Counts	Char	Counts
1	19	e	2356	p	5693
2	11	f	2153	q	49
3	6	g	1506	r	1769
4	29	h	3475	s	5643
5	8	i	2984	t	3076
6	2	j	241	u	545
7	2	k	408	v	1155
a	4898	l	2274	w	430
b	2193	m	3620	x	143
c	5447	n	2690	y	35
d	4583	o	1268	z	63

Table 2: Counts for each starting character of all MeSH terms

Level two of the MeSH term index tree represents the number of tokens for each MeSH entry term. A token in a normalized MeSH term can be a single character, number, or letter. The distribution for the token count in all MeSH entry terms is given in Table 3. Even the bin with the maximum number of tokens still contains 210 normalized MeSH entry terms. Here, the counts follow a broadly skewed distribution.

Num	Counts	Num	Counts	Num	Counts
1	2730	6	2625	11	210
2	2835	7	1995	12	315
3	3150	8	1470	13	105
4	3465	9	840	14	210
5	2835	10	630		

Table 3: Counts for number of tokens in a term

For level three of the MeSH term index tree the distribution is given as a graph in Figure 4. This level encodes the string length of the MeSH entry terms. Again, the distribution is broad, this time nearly Gaussian.

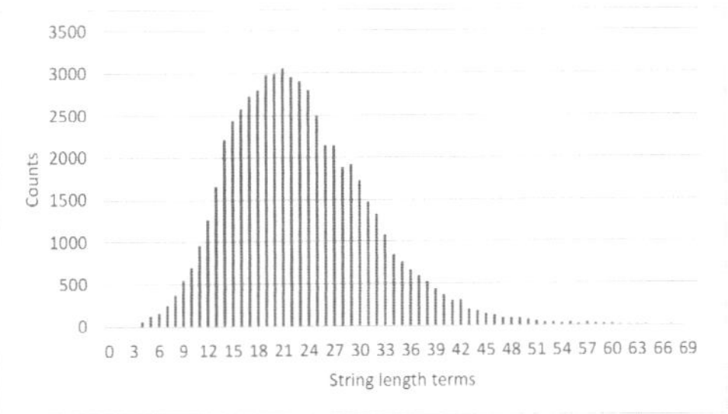

Figure 4: Length distribution of MeSH terms

In level four of the MeSH term index tree it is revealed that the divide and conquer strategy of the index tree was successful. The histogram in Table 4 shows the distribution for the number of MeSH entry terms in the leaf nodes of the index tree. In the first bin the list size is 1 for 1'002 leaf nodes, in the second bin the list size is between 2 and 5 for 871 leaf nodes. So, the majority of leaf nodes contains small lists.

Min bin	1	2	5	10	20	50
Max bin	2	5	10	20	50	150
Counts	1'002	871	512	392	379	310

Table 4: Histogram of the number of terms in a list

5.2. Results tagging fourteen million PubMed records

The corpus to index contained fourteen million (14'138'576) PubMed records. These were records which were previously found by querying PubMed for gene names. Only twelve million records contained a summary, additionally to the title. The number of tokens indexed by Lucene summed up to 2.8 billion tokens. MeSH term indexing for all records took around three days with a performance of around 4'000 records per minute. A file was compiled which listed all disease MeSH terms together with the PubMed identifiers where this disease term was found (*diseaseList*). A sample of 10'000 indexed PubMed records was analyzed for detail. The sample was drawn from *diseaseList* by random sampling technique with a limit of ten records per disease. Resulting, the 10'000 records represented 1'056 diseases from *diseaseList*. All records contained at least one disease MeSH term from the MeSH term index tree. In total, 61'413 MeSH terms were found by the MeSH term index tree. For 857 records no MeSH term was retrieved from PubMed. A sum of 25'982 MeSH terms was retrieved from PubMed. The MeSH term index tree did not tag 3'387 of these MeSH terms. The results were summarized in Table 5. The result file for the 10'000 records is available on request from the author.

MeSH terms	Found	Not found	Overlap
PubMed	25'982	38'818	22'595
Index tree	61'413	3'387	

Table 5: Counts for MeSH terms found in 10'000 PubMed records. Index tree for 'MeSH term index tree'

These results revealed a high discrepancy between the indexing by the NIH and the MeSH term index tree. So, we took a close look to single records. After sorting the 10'000 sample records by disease terms the first disease term was 'Abdomen, Acute'. The first record had the title 'Patient factors influencing the effect of surgeon-performed ultrasound on the acute abdomen', PubMed Id 21290005, from year 2010 in Critical Ultrasound Journal. No PubMed MeSH terms were given. The MeSH term index tree indexed the record with the disease MeSH terms 'Abdomen, Acute', 'Abdominal Pain', 'Appendicitis', and 'Peritonitis'. As it can be taken from the record summary in InfoBox 1 all terms occur in the text.

An example with overlap between the two indexing methods and where the NIH indexing exclusively tagged a MeSH term is record PID 18294294. The PubMed MeSH terms 'Leukemia, Lymphoid', and 'Recurrence' were not tagged by the MeSH term index tree. Both methods found 'Lymphoma, Extranodal NK-T-Cells' in the text. The MeSH term index tree tagged exclusively the record with 'Dis-

PURPOSE: To evaluate the effect of surgeon-performed ultrasound on acute abdomen in specific patient subgroups regarding the diagnostic accuracy and further management. METHODS: Eight hundred patients attending the emergency department at Stockholm South General Hospital, Sweden, for abdominal pain, were randomized to either receive or not receive surgeon-performed ultrasound as a complement to routine management. Patients were divided into subgroups based on patient characteristics. [...] Timing of surgery was evaluated for patients with peritonitis. [...] Decreased need for further examinations and/or fewer admissions were seen in all groups except in patients with a preliminary diagnosis of appendicitis. [...]

InfoBox 1: Part of summary for PubMed record with Id 21290005

ease Resistance', 'Glycogen Storage Disease Type VI', 'Leukemia', 'Leukemia, large Granular Lymphocytic', 'Lymphoma', 'Lymphoproliferative Disorders', 'Neoplasms', 'Neutropenia', 'Precursor T-Cell Lymphoblastic Leukemia-Lymphoma', and 'Sepsis'. Obviously, 'Leukemia, Lymphoid' is a meta term, given from the NIH index crew. And the NIH index crew skipped the leaf node tags 'Leukemia, large Granular Lymphocytic' and 'Precursor T-Cell Lymphoblastic Leukemia-Lymphoma'. Also not considered by the NIH were the meta tags 'Leukemia', 'Lymphoma', and 'Neoplasms'. The NIH summarized these tags with the meta tags. And our MeSH term index tree missed these meta tags, because no lexicographic matching pattern was found in the PubMed record. The two terms 'Sepsis' and 'Neutropenia' found from the MeSH term index tree were not tagged by the NIH. Presumably, because the tags are related to only one patient out of six. However, neutropenia, sepsis and chemotherapy have a causal relation (Ba et al., 2020). But if we are searching the PubMed MeSH terms for relations between neoplasms, sepsis, and neutropenia we will miss this publication.

6. Summary and conclusions

A new method to index PubMed records exhaustively with disease MeSH terms was developed and applied to a corpus of 14 million PubMed records. A random sample with 10'000 indexed records was analyzed in detail. In this sample 8.6% of the records were not indexed in PubMed. Why so many records were not indexed by the NIH, is under examination. Additionally, the MeSH term index tree found 2.4 times more MeSH terms than given in the PubMed records. This can partly explain that the NIH indexing aims to index with the most meaningful tags. And, the NIH indexing crew summarizes concepts with MeSH terms that are closer to the root of the MeSH term index tree. These summarizing MeSH terms explain the ten percent of the MeSH terms in PubMed that were not tagged by the MeSH term index tree. The NIH indexing includes a ranking of concepts, our approach is unbiased. Together, the two systems provide a large basis for information extraction from PubMed. Thus, in future work, the combination of the two index systems will be tested as input for machine learning systems to find new relations between diseases. The MeSH term index tree is highly precise, it only accepts records that match entry MeSH terms that were defined by the NIH. Our approach is unbiased. It does not need any training records. Only a minimum set of parameters is needed. Rough mismatches were excluded by defining the list of false similar terms. False similar term pairs are lexicographically similar but possess a different meaning. Also, common words are excluded from matching. The few parameters and very general rules make our algorithm highly reliable. The four level MeSH term index tree is very well balanced, this results in a very high indexing performance. We are convinced that our algorithm supports the scientific community in indexing life science literature and plan to provide the source code as open source project on git hub.

7. Bibliographical References

Aho, A. V. and Corasick, M. J. (1975). Efficient string matching: an aid to bibliographic search. *Communications of the ACM*, 18(6):333–340.

Aronson, A. R. and Lang, F.-M. (2010). An overview of metamap: historical perspective and recent advances. *Journal of the American Medical Informatics Association*, 17(3):229–236.

Ba, Y., Shi, Y., Jiang, W., Feng, J., Cheng, Y., Xiao, L., Zhang, Q., Qiu, W., Xu, B., Xu, R., et al. (2020). Current management of chemotherapy-induced neutropenia in adults: key points and new challenges: committee of neoplastic supportive-care (cons), china anti-cancer association committee of clinical chemotherapy, china anti-cancer association. *Cancer Biology & Medicine*, 17(4):896.

Białecki, A., Muir, R., Ingersoll, G., and Imagination, L. (2012). Apache lucene 4. In *SIGIR 2012 workshop on open source information retrieval*, page 17.

Dai, S., You, R., Lu, Z., Huang, X., Mamitsuka, H., and Zhu, S. (2020). Fullmesh: improving large-scale mesh indexing with full text. *Bioinformatics*, 36(5):1533–1541.

Díaz, N. P. C. and López, M. J. M. (2015). An analysis of biomedical tokenization: problems and strategies. In *Proceedings of the Sixth International Workshop on Health Text Mining and Information Analysis*, pages 40–49.

Funk, M. E. and Reid, C. A. (1983). Indexing consistency in medline. *Bulletin of the Medical Library Association*, 71(2):176.

Gargiulo, F., Silvestri, S., Ciampi, M., and De Pietro, G. (2019). Deep neural network for hierarchical extreme multi-label text classification. *Applied Soft Computing*, 79:125–138.

Hadfield, R. M. (2020). Delay and bias in pubmed medical subject heading (mesh) indexing of respiratory journals. *medRxiv*.

Huang, M., Névéol, A., and Lu, Z. (2011). Recommending mesh terms for annotating biomedical articles. *Journal of the American Medical Informatics Association*, 18(5):660–667.

Irwin, A. N. and Rackham, D. (2017). Comparison of the time-to-indexing in pubmed between biomedical journals according to impact factor, discipline, and focus. *Research in Social and Administrative Pharmacy*, 13(2):389–393.

Kaufman, J. (2017). Most common english words. `https://github.com/first20hours/google-10000-english`.

Leaman, R., Islamaj Doğan, R., and Lu, Z. (2013). Dnorm: disease name normalization with pairwise learning to rank. *Bioinformatics*, 29(22):2909–2917.

Lipscomb, C. E. (2000). Medical subject headings (mesh). *Bulletin of the Medical Library Association*, 88(3):265.

Liu, K., Peng, S., Wu, J., Zhai, C., Mamitsuka, H., and Zhu, S. (2015). Meshlabeler: improving the accuracy of large-scale mesh indexing by integrating diverse evidence. *Bioinformatics*, 31(12):i339–i347.

Mao, Y. and Lu, Z. (2017). Mesh now: automatic mesh indexing at pubmed scale via learning to rank. *Journal of biomedical semantics*, 8(1):1–9.

NIH. (2022a). Mesh tree. `https://nlmpubs.nlm.nih.gov/projects/mesh/MESH_FILES/meshtrees/`.

NIH. (2022b). Pubmed entry site. `https://pubmed.ncbi.nlm.nih.gov/`.

NIH. (2022). Medical subject headings. `https://www.nlm.nih.gov/bsd/disted/meshtutorial/introduction/02.html`.

Ruch, P., Gobeill, J., Lovis, C., and Geissbühler, A. (2008). Automatic medical encoding with snomed categories. In *BMC medical informatics and decision making*, volume 8, pages 1–8. BioMed Central.

Schulz, K. U. and Mihov, S. (2002). Fast string correction with levenshtein automata. *International Journal on Document Analysis and Recognition*, 5(1):67–85.

Swanson, D. R., Smalheiser, N. R., and Torvik, V. I. (2006). Ranking indirect connections in literature-based discovery: The role of medical subject headings. *Journal of the American society for information science and technology*, 57(11):1427–1439.

Wei, C.-H., Kao, H.-Y., and Lu, Z. (2013). Pubtator: a web-based text mining tool for assisting biocuration. *Nucleic acids research*, 41(W1):W518–W522.

World Health Organization. (2016). International classification of diseases. 2016. `https://www.who.int/standards/classifications/classification-of-diseases`.

UDeasy: a Tool for Querying Treebanks in CoNLL-U Format

Luca Brigada Villa
University of Bergamo / Pavia
luca.brigadavilla@unibg.it

Abstract

Many tools are available to query a dependency treebank, but they require the users to know a query language. This paper presents UDeasy, an application whose main goal is to allow the users to easily query and extract patterns from a dependency treebank in CoNLL-U format. To do this, users are prompted in a series of dialogs to enter relevant information about syntactic nodes, their properties, relationship, and positions.

Keywords: dependency treebanks, query tool

1. Introduction

CoNLL-U is the standard format for the annotation of dependency treebanks in many frameworks such as Universal Dependencies (UD) (de Marneffe et al., 2021) and Surface Syntactic Universal Dependencies (SUD) (Gerdes et al., 2018). It is a revised version of the CoNLL-X format (Buchholz and Marsi, 2006) and consists of ten fields separated by single tab characters carrying information about the morphology and the syntax of each token.

In this paper, I present UDeasy, a tool whose goal is to make it easy to design a query for treebanks annotated in CoNLL-U format. The paper is structured as follows: in Section 2, I list some of the available tools for processing and querying treebanks annotated in CoNLL-U format; in Section 3, I present UDeasy and how to use it; finally, Section 4 contains a summary of the advantages of using UDeasy for quantitative linguistic research.

2. Tools

Among the available tools that allow querying a dependency treebank, it is worth to mention CoNLL-U viewer, UDAPI, TüNDRA and Grew-match. I will discuss them in more detail pointing out the advantages and disadvantages of their use.

2.1. CoNLL-U viewer

CoNLL-U viewer (developed by Milan Straka and Michal Sedlák)[1] is a browser-based visualization tool for CoNLL-U files. It shows the trees representing the sentences stored in a CoNLL-U file uploaded by the users and allows downloading the generated image files.

2.2. UDAPI

UDAPI (Popel et al., 2017) is an API for processing Universal Dependencies. It is available in Python, Perl and Java as a library and, in addition, it can be used from the command-line interface. It allows the users to do operations such as parsing sentences, visualizing trees both in ASCII and HTML, querying treebanks and convert from one format to another.

2.3. TüNDRA

TüNDRA (Martens, 2013) is a web application for querying and visualizing treebanks. It allows to access more than 400 treebanks (most of them dependency treebanks) already available on the website and lets users upload their own treebanks in TCF or CoNLL-U format. Its query language is based on the TIGERSearch language (König and Lezius, 2003). In addition, TüNDRA allows the users to gather statistical information about the results of a query.

2.4. Grew-match

Grew-match (Guillaume, 2021) is a web application for searching graph patterns in treebanks in projects such as Universal Dependencies, Surface Syntax Universal Dependencies, French Sequoia corpus (Candito and Seddah, 2012), three corpora in AMR (Banarescu et al., 2013) and MultiWord Expression annotation from the Parseme project (Ramisch et al., 2020). Grew-match has also an offline version which can be used to query patterns from treebanks owned by the users.

3. UDeasy

UDeasy is an application written in Python 3 with a graphic interface built using the GUI toolkit wxPython[2]. The functions to extract the occurrences from a treebank rely on the udapi Python package (Popel et al., 2017). It has been developed to work on Windows, MacOS and Linux systems. It is licensed under a Creative Commons Attribution-NonCommercial-ShareAlike 4.0 International License and published at https://unipv-larl.github.io/udeasy/.

3.1. Why UDeasy

When using one of the applications or tools mentioned earlier, a user may encounter some issues:

[1] https://universaldependencies.org/conllu_viewer.html

[2] see http://wxPython.org/

- some of the tools only allow querying treebanks that are hosted online and not uploaded by the users (e.g. Grew-match online)
- some of the tools are designed to be used from a command line interface or included in a script (e.g. UDAPI)
- all the tools force the users to learn a query language

These factors may complicate the work of a linguist who wants to follow a quantitative and data-driven approach.
The goal of UDeasy is to overcome these issues by allowing the users to extract patterns from dependency treebanks with a simplified process. The main advantages of using UDeasy are the following:

- it accepts all the treebanks that are formatted in CoNLL-U
- it has a graphical interface that guides the users step by step in the design of the query
- there is no need to learn any query language

3.2. How to use UDeasy

The tool is designed as a series of panels dedicated to the different parameters that the users may want to set in order to extract a pattern from a treebank. When opening the application, a window pops up and the users are asked to select a CoNLL-U file stored on their computer.

3.2.1. Naming the nodes

When clicking on the button to confirm the selection of the CoNLL-U file, the nodes panel appears. The users are asked to give a name to the nodes that are involved in the target pattern. The names are not part of the actual query, but they will be used to refer to the target nodes in the subsequent steps.

3.2.2. Selecting the features for each target node

In the panel that appears, the users can indicate one or more features that the target nodes involved in the pattern must match. The users can select any of the CoNLL-U fields (`lemma`, `upos`, `deprel`) or any of the sub-features that some CoNLL-U fields have such as `feats` and `misc`.
As values for the selected features, the users can either enter one or more values that have to be matched. If the users enter a value, then the feature must have that exact value for the node if the parameter `value is` is selected; if more values are passed, they have to be written between squared brackets and separated by commas. If the feature has one of those values, then the node is included in the results.
In the feature dropdown menu, the users will find all the CoNLL-U fields and some of the sub-features of `feats` and `misc`: if they want to look for a sub-feature not included in the menu, they can insert the value with the keyboard.

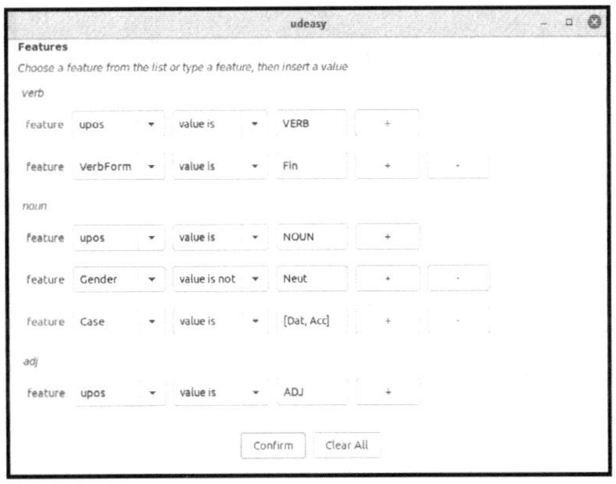

Figure 1: The features panel how it appears in the application; *verb*, *noun* and *adj* are the names given to the nodes in the previous stage (see Section 3.2.1).

3.2.3. Specifying the relations among nodes

In order to specify the relations among the nodes, the users can select from the dropdown menu in the relations panel the nodes (using the names given to the target nodes in the first panel - see Section 3.2.1) and a relation selected from `is parent of`, `is ancestor of` and `is sibling of`.

3.2.4. Specifying the relative positions among nodes

The last parameter the users might want to specify is the relative positions of the nodes. Like the relations, the conditions for the relative positions must involve two nodes. If the users do not want to specify any ordering among the nodes, they can leave the fields empty. Otherwise, they must give a value for the first three fields, i.e. the nodes and the ordering relation (`precedes` or `follows`). In addition to that, they can specify a distance between the nodes selecting either `by exactly` or `by at least` in the fourth field and entering an integer number.

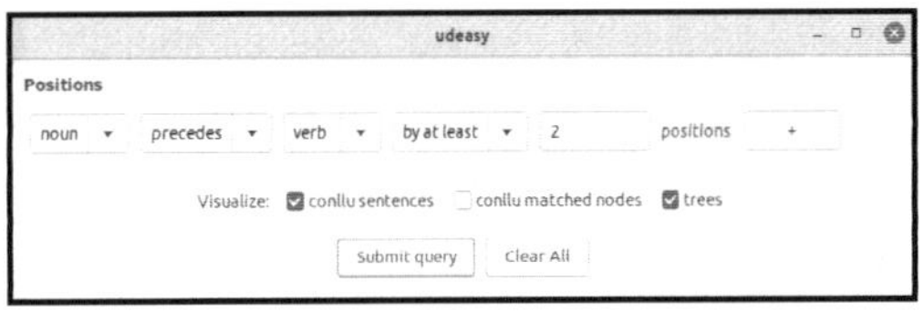

Figure 2: The positions panel as it appears in the application.

3.2.5. Results

As shown in Figure 2, the users can select some visualization options such as `conllu sentences`, `conllu matched nodes` and `trees` according to whether they want to see in the results the sentences that have at least a matched pattern formatted in

CoNLL-U, the nodes involved in the matched patterns and the trees of such sentences.
According to what the users have selected, the results will appear in a new window after clicking the button `Submit query`.

3.2.6. Statistics

In the window where the results appear, the users will see an option named `Stats` which allows getting some statistical information about the patterns matched by the submitted query such as word order, distances among the nodes and the distribution of the values of features.

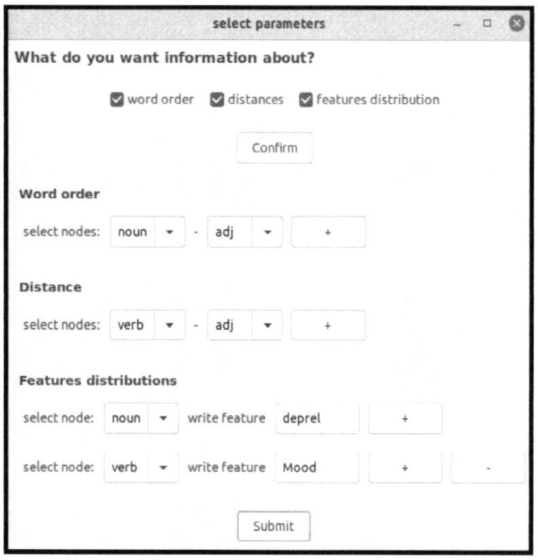

Figure 3: The statistics panel as it appears in the application.

For example, considering the parameters shown in Figure 3, the users will obtain the ordering of the nodes they named *noun* and *adj*, the distribution of the distances between the nodes *verb* and *adj* along with their average distance in the matched sentences and the distribution of the selected features of the nodes *noun* and *verb*.

Mood	count	frequency
Ind	219	0.706452
Sub	85	0.274194
Imp	6	0.0193548

Figure 4: The table showing the values of the feature *Mood*.

For the case of the feature *Mood*, the output will be a table showing all the possible values this feature can take with their frequency in the results, as shown in Figure 4.

4. Conclusion and Future Work

As shown in Section 3, UDeasy is a user-friendly tool that can be used without any knowledge of programming or query languages. I believe it would be a useful tool for the community of linguists who want to use a data-driven approach and for the students who approach dependency treebanks without almost any experience with queries.
Future work might include the implementation of additional features such as new visualization options for the results or new statistics obtainable by the users. Additionally, UDeasy may be upgraded allowing the users to process treebanks formatted in CoNLL-U Plus[3] and to include regular expressions in their queries.

5. Bibliographical References

Banarescu, L., Bonial, C., Cai, S., Georgescu, M., Griffitt, K., Hermjakob, U., Knight, K., Koehn, P., Palmer, M., and Schneider, N. (2013). Abstract Meaning Representation for sembanking. In *Proceedings of the 7th Linguistic Annotation Workshop and Interoperability with Discourse*, pages 178–186, Sofia, Bulgaria, August. Association for Computational Linguistics.

Buchholz, S. and Marsi, E. (2006). CoNLL-X shared task on multilingual dependency parsing. In *Proceedings of the Tenth Conference on Computational Natural Language Learning (CoNLL-X)*, pages 149–164, New York City, June. Association for Computational Linguistics.

Candito, M. and Seddah, D. (2012). Le corpus Sequoia : annotation syntaxique et exploitation pour l'adaptation d'analyseur par pont lexical. In *TALN 2012 - 19e conférence sur le Traitement Automatique des Langues Naturelles*, Grenoble, France, June.

de Marneffe, M.-C., Manning, C. D., Nivre, J., and Zeman, D. (2021). Universal Dependencies. *Computational Linguistics*, 47(2):255–308, 07.

Gerdes, K., Guillaume, B., Kahane, S., and Perrier, G. (2018). SUD or Surface-Syntactic Universal Dependencies: An annotation scheme near-isomorphic to UD. In *Universal Dependencies Workshop 2018*, Brussels, Belgium, November.

Guillaume, B. (2021). Graph matching and graph rewriting: GREW tools for corpus exploration, maintenance and conversion. In *Proceedings of the 16th Conference of the European Chapter of the Association for Computational Linguistics: System Demonstrations*, pages 168–175, Online, April. Association for Computational Linguistics.

König, E. and Lezius, W., (2003). *TIGERSearch User's Manual IMS*. University of Stuttgart, Stuttgart, Germany.

Martens, S. (2013). Tündra: A Web Application for Treebank Search and Visualization. In *Proceedings*

[3]https://universaldependencies.org/ext-format.html

of The Twelfth Workshop on Treebanks and Linguistic Theories (TLT12), pages 133–144, Sofia, Bulgaria, December.

Popel, M., Žabokrtský, Z., and Vojtek, M. (2017). Udapi: Universal API for Universal Dependencies. In *Proceedings of the NoDaLiDa 2017 Workshop on Universal Dependencies (UDW 2017)*, pages 96–101, Gothenburg, Sweden, May. Association for Computational Linguistics.

Ramisch, C., Savary, A., Guillaume, B., Waszczuk, J., Candito, M., Vaidya, A., Barbu Mititelu, V., Bhatia, A., Iñurrieta, U., Giouli, V., Güngör, T., Jiang, M., Lichte, T., Liebeskind, C., Monti, J., Ramisch, R., Stymne, S., Walsh, A., and Xu, H. (2020). Edition 1.2 of the PARSEME shared task on semi-supervised identification of verbal multiword expressions. In *Proceedings of the Joint Workshop on Multiword Expressions and Electronic Lexicons*, pages 107–118, online, December. Association for Computational Linguistics.

Matrix and Double-Array Representations for Efficient Finite State Tokenization

Nils Diewald
Leibniz Institute for the German Language
Mannheim, Germany
diewald@ids-mannheim.de

Abstract

This paper presents an algorithm and an implementation for efficient tokenization of texts of space-delimited languages based on a deterministic finite state automaton. Two representations of the underlying data structure are presented and a model implementation for German is compared with state-of-the-art approaches. The presented solution is faster than other tools while maintaining comparable quality.

Keywords: Tokenization, Finite State, Corpora

1. Introduction

Tokenization, i.e. the segmentation of a text string into "distinct meaningful units" (Kaplan, 2005) is a fundamental step in the preparation of linguistic corpora. Character sequences are subdivided (like "Look␣it␣up ␣at␣p.␣124!␣;-)" into "Look|it|up|at|p.|124|!|;-)|") to make the individual units accessible for search engines and further linguistic analysis. Since errors in tokenization often have a significant impact on further processing and analyses, high accuracy is of great importance. As ambiguities concerning sentence boundaries have to be resolved for tokenization, they are usually marked in the same step.

Although tokenization – especially for space-delimited languages such as English or German – is considered one of the simpler applications of natural language processing (NLP) and is often regarded as a solved problem, there are some cases where programmatic recognition of token boundaries pose challenges and naïve approaches may fail, for example, in distinguishing the period character at the end of an abbreviation from marking the end of a sentence. More recent phenomena of computer-mediated communication (CMC), such as emoticons, URLs, or email addresses, pose difficulties in particular.

Tokenization is rarely a time-critical process, especially in preprocessing for much more time-consuming syntactic or semantic analyses. And the quality of the results is clearly the most important measure for evaluating this task. However, in the case of very large corpora in research data preparation, tokenization can be challenging – and speed of processing, accompanied by low resource consumption, can be an important criterion in deciding which tool to choose.

In many areas of NLP, rule-based approaches have been replaced by machine-learning (ML) methods in recent years. This is due to more efficient algorithms and better hardware for the implementation of such solutions on the one hand, and to the availability of large

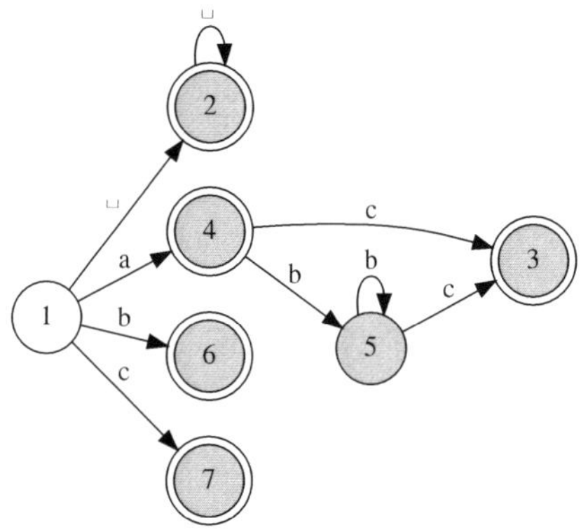

Figure 1: Lexical analyzer for tokens a, b, c, ab^*c and whitespace sequences (␣$^+$).

annotated corpora for training these systems on the other hand. Tokenization and sentence segmentation are still exceptions to this (although there are significant differences with respect to different languages). The main reason is that accuracy of rule-based tokenizers for space-delimited languages is already very high. For German, for example, rule-based approaches continue to outperform ML approaches significantly both in terms of accuracy and speed (Ortmann et al., 2019; Diewald et al., 2022).

1.1. Lexical Analyzers

Rule-based tokenizers and sentence segmenters have traditionally been based on *lexical analyzers* (Aho et al., 2007, ch. 3) using a general purpose lexical scanner generator such as Lex (Lesk and Schmidt, 1975) or modern successor systems like Flex, JFlex or Ragel. Rules for lexical units are formulated as regular expressions and transformed into a deterministic finite state automaton (FSA), which linearly searches the input stream, executes arbitrary code when reaching terminal states, and for ambiguous inputs follows the principle

Proceedings of the CMLC-10 Workshop (@LREC 2022), pages 20–26
Marseille, 20 June 2022

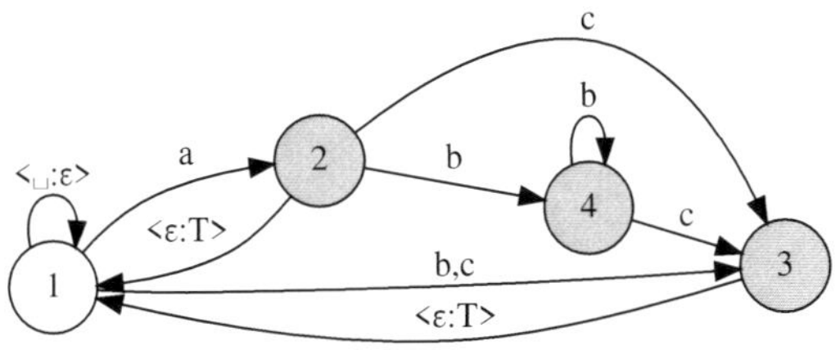

Figure 2: Tokenizing automaton segmenting a, b, c, ab*c, ignoring whitespace sequences ($\textvisiblespace^{+}$) and introducing token boundaries (T).

of the longest match (see Fig. 1).

Modern rule-based tokenizers also follow this approach, for example the Stanford Tokenizer[1], BlingFire[2], or KorAP-Tokenizer[3] (Kupietz and Diewald, 2020). Tokenizers that rely on dictionaries to vectorize an input stream follow a similar approach (Song et al., 2021).

1.2. Finite State Transducers

An alternative – or generalization – of this approach is the tokenization using finite state transducers (FST; Beesley and Karttunen, 2003, ch. 9.2; Beesley, 2004). FSTs are finite state automata with translating edges. They not only accept symbol sequences of an input string, but return for each input symbol an output symbol and thus generate for each accepted input string at least one output string. By supporting empty characters (ε) in input and output, i.e. symbols which do not consume or produce any characters, it is possible to formulate a transducer that converts an input stream into an arbitrarily segmented output stream (see Fig. 2).

Kaplan (2005) describes an algorithm based on an FST representation of a tokenizer. Following a breadth-first traversal, an incremental composition operation is performed on the tokenizing FST with a linear text FSA. The output of the operation is an FSA of all possible tokenizations (or a sequence of these FSAs), with the ambiguities still intact to be resolved by higher-level lexical constraints.

1.3. Further Models

Further approaches of rule-based tokenizers extend these models, for example, to a list of finite state automata that are applied in a defined order (Proisl and Uhrig, 2016), or by applying context-free rules recursively (Graën et al., 2018, or SpaCy[4]).

[1]http://nlp.stanford.edu/software/tokenizer.shtml
[2]https://github.com/Microsoft/BlingFire
[3]https://github.com/KorAP/KorAP-Tokenizer
[4]https://spacy.io/usage/linguistic-features#tokenization

2. Data Structure

While Lex-like scanner generators allow arbitrary code executions at terminal nodes, and FSTs support arbitrary character transitions, for a finite state tokenizer the transition types can be reduced to three cases:

Identity: The input symbol corresponds to the output symbol (e.g., a character within a word);

Deletion: The input symbol can be ignored (e.g., a whitespace character between word boundaries);

Token Boundary: The input symbol is followed by the end of a token (e.g., a dot at the end of an abbreviation).

Beesley (2004) proposes a mechanism for formulating an FST-based tokenizer, which inserts a transition following every acceptable token, which consumes an empty character (i.e., can always be traversed) and produces a token boundary marker (T). The above rules can then be mapped to three types of edges in the automaton (see Fig. 2 for an application of these rules):

$<?>$	for the identical output of arbitrary input symbols;
$<? : \varepsilon>$	for the deletion of arbitrary input symbols;
$<\varepsilon : T>$	for marking token boundaries without consuming an input symbol.

Compared to an FSA or FST, terminal nodes do not play a role in finite state tokenizers – the set of terminal nodes is empty. We can represent it accordingly as a quintuple:

Σ	Finite alphabet of the input language ($\varepsilon \in \Sigma$);
Φ	Finite set of states;
δ	State transition function;
s_1	Initial state;
δ_D	Finite set of all $<? : \varepsilon>$ transitions.

Reducing the transducer to these simple rules guarantees, that for an input symbol to be consumed exactly one output symbol exists. Ambiguity with respect to token boundaries arises only when traversing $<\varepsilon : T>$.

2.1. Matrix Representation

A standard representation of all transitions of a finite state automaton is a state transition table (Tab. 1 shows the matrix representation of the automaton in Fig. 1). Additional information includes the initial state and terminal nodes.

A transducer would encode output symbols in addition to the destination node in this table. Due to the reduced transition types of the tokenizer, this can be simplified by encoding all identity transitions with a positive sign and all deletion transitions with a negative sign[5] (see

[5]In an implementation, the most-significant bit could be used for marking.

	s_1	s_2	s_3	s_4	s_5	s_6	s_7
a	4	0	0	0	0	0	0
b	6	0	0	5	5	0	0
c	7	0	0	3	3	0	0
␣	2	2	0	0	0	0	0

Table 1: State Transition Table for FSA of Fig. 1

	s_1	s_2	s_3	s_4
a	2	0	0	0
b	3	4	0	4
c	3	3	0	3
␣	-1	0	0	0
ε	0	1	1	0

Table 2: State Transition Table for the reduced FST of Fig. 2

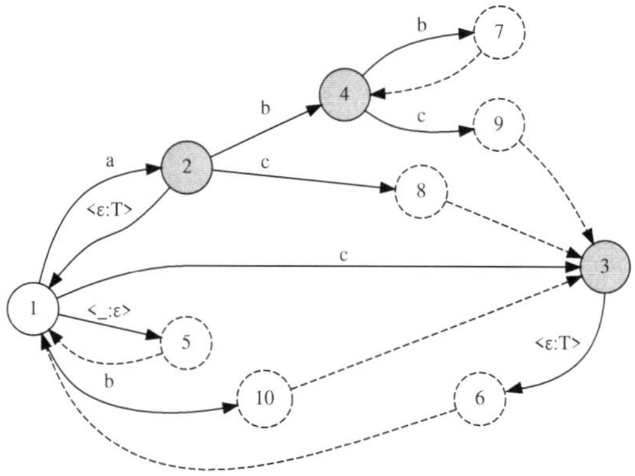

Figure 3: Double-array FST resembling the automaton in Fig. 2

Tab. 2, esp. $\delta(s_1, \text{␣}) = -1$ for an example of a deletion transition). Since ε transitions by definition only mark token boundaries (T) no additional encoding is necessary.

2.2. Double-Array Representation

However, the matrix representation can cause a problem: Not only the number of states in the automaton has an influence on the model size and thus on the required storage space, but also the size of the alphabet $|\Sigma|$. This can be an issue depending on the language to model and the sparseness of the transition table. Alternatively, the finite state tokenizer can be implemented based on a double-array (DA) trie (Aoe, 1989) as a DA finite state machine (Mizobuchi et al., 2000). In a DA trie the state transition function of an automaton can be represented in two one-dimensional numeric arrays of equal length (`base` and `check`). Both state and input symbols are encoded as numeric values > 0. A state transition $t_0 = \delta(t, x)$ is thereby valid if:

$$t_0 = \texttt{base}[t] + \texttt{code}[x]$$
$$\texttt{check}[t_0] = t$$

A target state is recorded in the `base` array at the position of the sum of the current state and the numeric code of the input symbol. In the construction of the DA trie[6] care is taken, that the transitions are stored compactly and possibly overlapping, therefore in the `check` array at the target position the parent state must be checked.

The difference between a trie and a regular FSA is that the in-degree of a state in the FSA can be > 1 and that circular structures may exist. While the representation as a DA allows for circular structures, it can not represent nodes with an in-degree > 1. Mizobuchi et al. (2000) therefore introduce groups of "separate states" for nodes that have an in-degree > 1, pointing to a "representative state" to encode FSAs in DA structures (Fig. 3 shows the automaton from Fig. 2 with separate states in dashed circles pointing to representative states). To model the relationship of separate states to representative states in the DA, they introduce an intermediate step in the `base` array, which encodes with a negative sign. If `base`$[t]$ has a negative sign, the transition corresponds to a separate state whose value points to the representative state. Accordingly, in addition to the condition above, the following is true:

$$t_t = \texttt{base}[t] + \texttt{code}[x]$$
$$t_0 = \begin{Bmatrix} \texttt{base}[|t_t|],\ if\ t_t < 0 \\ t_t,\ otherwise \end{Bmatrix}$$

When traversing the edges, this intermediate step must be taken into account.

Corresponding to this mechanism, $<?:\varepsilon>$ edges can be represented in the double array to model a finite state tokenizer, in that for transitions with the destination t the value in `check`$[t_0]$ is given a negative sign. Note, that this check must be performed before the resolution of a separate state (Tab. 3 shows one possible representation of the automaton in Fig. 3 as an extended DA FSA with representative state references and deleting transitions).

As this representation is independent of $|\Sigma|$, it can lead to smaller models under certain conditions.

3. Algorithm

Algorithm 1 shows the simplified (see below) tokenization of an input sequence in into the tokenized output sequence out. The algorithm is representation-agnostic, the only difference to be noted is that with a DA representation, the sign of the target node comes from the `check` and the value corresponds to the representative state from `base`.

Valid transitions: For each input character in_i the transition $\delta(t, in_i)$ is checked in the automaton. Characters leading to targets with a positive sign are written

[6]Regarding the efficient construction of static DA tries, please refer to Niu et al. (2013).

	t_1	t_2	t_3	t_4	t_5	t_6	t_7	t_8	t_9	t_{10}
`base`	1	4	-3	3	-1	8	-3	-1	-1	-6
`check`	10	1	1	1	-1	2	2	4	2	6

Table 3: Extended double-array FSA of Fig. 3, with `code[a]`=1, `code[b]`=2, `code[c]`=3, `code[␣]`=4, `code[ε]`=5. The length of the DA is stored in `check[1]`.

Algorithm 1: Main tokenization loop

Input: *in* is a character stream

Output: *out* is a tokenized character stream

```
1  newChar ← true;
2  i ← 0; // position in in
3  j ← 0; // position in out
4  t_ε ← 0 (≠ s_1); i_ε ← 0; j_ε ← 0; t ← s_1;
5  while i < |in| do
6      if newChar then
7          char ← in_i;
8          if char ∉ Σ then char ←?;
9          t_0 ← t;
10         if δ(t_0, ε) ≠ 0 then t_ε ← t_0; i_ε ← i;
             j_ε ← j;
11     t ← δ(t_0, char);
12     if t = 0 then
13         if char ≠ ε and t_ε ≠ 0 then
14             t_0 ← t_ε; i ← i_ε; j ← j_ε; char ← ε;
15         else
16             if t_o = s_1 then
17                 i ← i + 1; out_j ← in_i;
18             else
19                 t_0 ← s_1;
20             out_j ← T; j ← j + 1;
                 newChar ← true;
21             restartLoop
22         newChar ← false
23         restartLoop
24     if char = ε then
25         out_j ← T; j ← j + 1;
26     else
27         i ← i + 1;
28         if t > 0 then
29             out_j ← char; j ← j + 1;
                 newChar ← true;
30     if t < 0 then t ← −t;
31     newChar ← true;
```

unchanged to the output stream (see line 28f). Characters that lead to targets with a negative sign are consumed only.

Backtracking: $<\varepsilon : T>$ edges allow a transition in the automaton without consuming a character of the input stream. This means that whenever a transition $\delta(t, in_i)$ is available, a possible transition $\delta(t, \varepsilon)$ must also be considered (cf. δ(2,b) in Fig. 2). Since this by definition implies a token boundary mark T, this can be used for backtracking semantics to follow a longest-match strategy (Lesk and Schmidt, 1975): During traversion, the last available $<\varepsilon : T>$ transition is remembered (see line 10), but character consumption is always prioritized. If a character cannot be consumed during traversion, the system repositions out and in, jumps to the last $<\varepsilon : T>$ source state (see line 13–14), traverses it, and continues.

Invalid transitions: If no valid transition of an input symbol exists and backtracking is not possible, a token boundary marker T is added to the output stream and the remaining input stream is continued from the initial state s_1 of the tokenizer. If the automaton is already initial, a character is consumed beforehand (see lines 15–21). This guarantees robust output of all input data with all automata. In carefully designed tokenizers, this behavior is rarely triggered.

The representation of the algorithm is simplified in that an implementation (and also the model) must be able to handle characters $\notin \Sigma$. In addition, special treatments are necessary with respect to the end of the processing. By concatenating several token boundary markers T, it is also possible to mark sentence boundaries (see Sec. 4.2).

The worst time complexity of the algorithm is $O(nm)$, where $n = |in|$ and m is the maximum path length excluding $<\varepsilon : T>$ edges. Intermediate memory requirement corresponds to the length of the text, whereby the processing can be handled by a buffer which can be flushed after each successfully parsed token.

4. Implementation

4.1. Datok

Datok (Diewald, 2022) is an implementation of a finite state tokenizer based on the aforementioned algorithm and datastructures. It is written in Go as a command line tool and was designed to be compatible with KorAP-Tokenizer.

Datok relies on XFST (Beesley and Karttunen, 2003) for the construction of its automaton in the free implementation of Foma (Hulden, 2009) (see next section; other FST toolkits should be equally suitable).

To create an automaton that can be interpreted by Datok, first Foma must compile the rule set into a compatible FST and subsequently Datok must convert the FST into a finite state tokenizer (optionally in matrix or DA representation). The final automaton can then be applied to arbitrary data input streams, and can output different forms of tokenization data (like new-line delimited surface forms or character offset information).

4.2. Construction

While the implementation of the algorithm and the underlying data structures are relatively simple, the complexity lies in the automaton and thus the challenge in its construction.

Rule creation in XFST essentially follows Beesley (2004), with the supplement to restrict rule formulation to valid transitions $<?>$, $<? : \varepsilon>$, and $<\varepsilon : T>$. The special symbol "@_TOKEN_BOUND_@" is introduced as the token bound marker.

A very simple tokenizer that follows the introduced rules, can be seen in Listing 1.

```
1  define TB "@_TOKEN_BOUND_@";
2  define WS [" "|"\u000a"|"\u0009"];
3  define PUNCT ["."|"?"|"!"];
4  define Char \[WS|PUNCT];
5  define Word Char+;
6
7  ! Compose token boundaries
8  define Tokenizer
9      [[Word|PUNCT] @-> ... TB] .o.
10 ! Compose Whitespace ignorance
11     [WS+ @-> 0] .o.
12 ! Compose sentence ends
13     [[PUNCT+] @-> ... TB \/ TB _ ];
14 read regex Tokenizer;
```

Listing 1: Compliant Tokenizer written in XFST

First, the token inventory of the tokenizer is defined using regular expressions (lines 1–5). The *direct replacement* operator "@->" (Karttunen, 1996), which performs a replacement on the longest possible path, and the context operator "...", which allows to insert arbitrary symbols around a match, are helpful for the creation of $<\varepsilon : T>$ transitions. In the example tokenizer these operators append the token boundary marker to the longest possible matches of all entries of the token inventory (line 9).

The $<? : \varepsilon>$ transitions are realized by replacing arbitrary characters with ε ("0" in XFST; used in the example for whitespace characters in line 11).

By using the direct replacement rules it is also possible to specify sequences of token boundary markers which can be interpreted separately by an implementation. For example, it is possible to mark sentence boundaries within the framework (line 13).

The *direct replacement* operations yields an unambiguous transducer for the unique processing of input streams. Unfortunately, such automata (especially in intermediate steps during compilation) can reach a very large size and thus require an enormous amount of resources. Due to the longest-match and backtracking strategy of the algorithm, however, it is possible to achieve unique outputs even with ambiguous transducers. Thus, when constructing the finite state tokenizer in XFST, automata of individual token inventories can first be created separately using direct replacement operators and then be unified, e.g., for the composition of sentence ending rules and whitespace treatment. This flexible construction of the tokenizer enables a tradeoff in terms of model size and processing speed (which decreases when backtracking is utilized to a great extent).

4.3. Benchmarks

In a real world tokenizer, these rules are more complex with respect to applicable contexts for token and sentence boundaries and the defined automata of the token inventory (e.g., abbreviation lists, emoticons, numbers). Datok (v0.1.5) contains a real world tokenizer for German with more than 18 thousand states, more than 2 million edges and $|\Sigma| = 167$. The ruleset is based on preliminary work by KorAP-Tokenizer and Çöltekin (2014). The matrix representation requires ~10.9 MB of memory, the DA representation ~18.5 MB (with a load factor[7] of ~70.8%).

Diewald et al. (2022) presents a detailed comparison of 15 different tools (both ML and rule based approaches) for the tokenization and sentence segmentation of German language data including Datok. Table 4 gives a summary of the results regarding the quality of Datok in the form of F_1 values with respect to tokenization and sentence segmentation in 3 different corpora: Version 2.9 of the German Universal Dependency GSD Corpus (McDonald et al., 2013) and the CMC and Web corpora of the EmpiriST Shared Task Challenge (Beißwenger et al., 2016). While all tested tools achieve values well above 99% for the tokenization of the UD-GSD corpus, the F_1 values for the CMC and Web corpora are comparatively very high.[8] The values for sentence segmentation are in the middle range.

	Tokens			Sentences
	UD-GSD	CMC	Web	UD-GSD
F_1	99.45%	98.79%	99.21%	97.60%

Table 4: Evaluation of the quality of Datok's sentence and token boundary detection for German (v0.1.5).

Figure 4 presents the performance in tokens per millisecond at different batch sizes (here logarithmically represented in $2^x \times 1000$ tokens) of four different tokenizers: Datok (in matrix and DA representation), BlingFire (as the fastest competitor tokenizer according to Diewald et al. 2022; v0.1.8 with the "wbd.bin" model using the Python API), KorAP-Tokenizer (v2.2.2), and Stanford Tokenizer (v4.4.0[9]; probably the most widely used tokenizer tool). The test

[7] I.e. the proportion of non-empty elements to all elements in the representation.

[8] For a detailed account of the evaluation, please refer to Diewald et al. (2022). The full evaluation suite including all results is available at `https://github.com/KorAP/Tokenizer-Evaluation`.

[9] Including sentence segmentation.

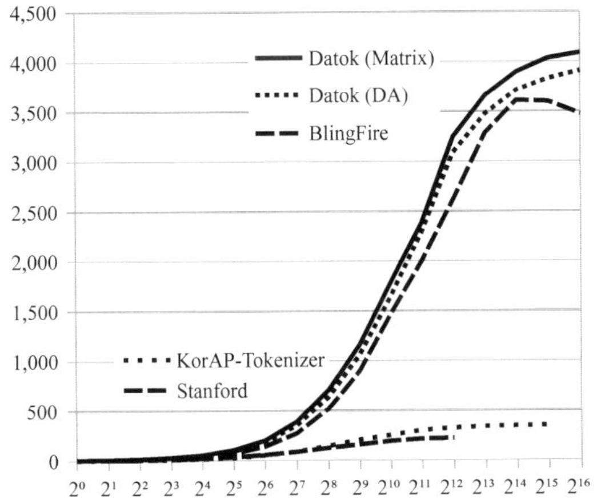

Figure 4: Benchmarks in t/ms for different batch sizes (averaged over 10 runs).

system is an Intel Xeon CPU E5-2630 v2 @ 2.60GHz with 12 cores and 64 GB of RAM. As can be seen, model loading and startup time has a big impact on very short texts but becomes negligible for longer texts.[10] Datok can process up to ~4,000 t/ms in matrix representation, ~3,900 t/ms in DA representation, and BlingFire ~3,600 t/ms. KorAP-Tokenizer (~350 t/ms) and Stanford Tokenizer (~220 t/ms) are significantly slower.

The implementation as a DA is slower than the matrix implementation (presumably due to the additional parent check for each traversion and the resolution of separate states), but still competitive and therefore a possible variant for implementations with large alphabets.

In view of the processing of very large corpora, such speed differences can play a significant role. Datok (like KorAP-Tokenizer) was primarily developed for tokenizing the German reference corpus DeReKo (Kupietz et al., 2018), which currently comprises over 50 billion tokens. Complete processing of this corpus on the test system would take ~13.5h using Datok (in matrix representation; assuming a batch size of 100,000 tokens and a single core), BlingFire ~33h, KorAP-Tokenizer ~8 days, and Stanford Tokenizer (including sentence segmentation) ~12.5 days. For the same task, some other tools require several years to complete and can therefore be considered impractical in this application scenario (Diewald et al., 2022).

5. Summary and Outlook

The algorithm and the corresponding data structures presented in this paper show a high performance in tokenizing large corpora in the implementation of Datok. At the same time, the model allows complex rule sets that achieve a very high quality for space-delimited languages. Thus, Datok can be used as a suitable tool in research data preparation.

However, there are some limitations associated with the algorithm that need to be taken into account. For example, long-distance relationships between tokens (Graën et al., 2018) cannot be used for disambiguation (e.g., opening single quotes that can help distinguish a closing single quote from being used as an apostrophe). Also, the left longest-match rule prevents valid tokens from being further subdivided, even though this may result in shorter segments on the right side of the analysis (e.g., the string "Go␣tohttp://google.com/", in which a space was omitted by mistake, would be tokenized using common word and URL rules into "Go|tohttp|:|/|/|google|.|com|/|" instead of "Go|to|http://google.com/|"). Since the output produced is unambiguous and no longer contains possible interpretations, ambiguities can not be resolved by higher-level lexical constraints (Kaplan, 2005).

Extensions to the algorithm and the data models are possible. Token boundaries could be marked to modify the backtracking behaviour (e.g., to exempt some ε edges from being considered as backtracking positions). And, specifically in matrix representation, token classes can be associated with token boundary markers (e.g., to additionally mark that a token is an URL), as is common in several tokenizer tools. This extension would also make it possible to resolve parts of the aforementioned restrictions by re-evaluating doubtful cases based on token classes in a second step.

Currently, Datok is in the evaluation phase for future use in tokenizing DeReKo, for which KorAP-Tokenizer is presently being used. Datok is open source[11] and published under the Apache 2.0 License. Language models for English and French are under preparation.

6. Bibliographical References

Aho, A. V., Lam, M. S., Sethi, R., and Ullman, J. D. (2007). *Compilers: Principles, Techniques, and Tools*. Pearson Education, Addison-Wesley, second edition.

Aoe, J.-I. (1989). A fast digital search algorithm using a double-array structure. *Systems and Computers in Japan*, 20(7):92–103.

Beesley, K. R. and Karttunen, L. (2003). *Finite State Morphology*. CSLI Studies in Computational Linguistics. CSLI Publications.

Beesley, K. R. (2004). Tokenizing Transducers. Technical report, Xerox Research Centre Europe, October.

Beißwenger, M., Bartsch, S., Evert, S., and Würzner, K.-M. (2016). EmpiriST 2015: A Shared Task on the Automatic Linguistic Annotation of Computer-Mediated Communication and Web Corpora. In *Proceedings of the 10th Web as Corpus Workshop*, pages 44–56, Berlin, August. Association for Computational Linguistics.

[10]Caching effects cannot be ruled out, since batches are based on a concatenated, repetitive text of ~98 thousand tokens.

[11]`https://github.com/KorAP/Datok`

Çöltekin, Ç. (2014). A set of open source tools for turkish natural language processing. In Nicoletta Calzolari, et al., editors, *Proceedings of the Ninth International Conference on Language Resources and Evaluation (LREC'14)*, pages 1079–1086, Reykjavik, Iceland. European Language Resources Association (ELRA).

Diewald, N., Kupietz, M., and Lüngen, H. (2022). Tokenizing on scale – Preprocessing large text corpora on the lexical and sentence level. In *Proceedings of EURALEX 2022*, Mannheim, Germany, July.

Diewald, N. (2022). Datok. Software; doi:10.5281/zenodo.6427259, `https://github.com/KorAP/Datok`.

Graën, J., Bertamini, M., and Volk, M. (2018). Cutter – a universal multilingual tokenizer. In Mark Cieliebak, et al., editors, *Swiss Text Analytics Conference*, number 2226 in CEUR Workshop Proceedings, pages 75–81. CEUR-WS, June.

Hulden, M. (2009). Foma: A finite-state toolkit and library. In *Proceedings of the 12th Conference of the European Chapter of the Association for Computational Linguistics*, pages 29–32.

Kaplan, R. M. (2005). A Method for Tokenizing Text. In Antti Arppe, et al., editors, *Inquiries into Words, Constraints and Contexts. Festschrift for Kimmo Koskenniemi on His 60th Birthday*, CSLI Studies in Computational Linguistics Online, pages 55–64. CSLI Publications, Ventura Hall.

Karttunen, L. (1996). Directed Replacement. In *34th Annual Meeting of the Association for Computational Linguistics*, pages 108–115, Santa Cruz, California, USA, June. Association for Computational Linguistics.

Kupietz, M. and Diewald, N. (2020). KorAP-Tokenizer. Software. doi:10.5281/zenodo.5040449, `https://github.com/KorAP/KorAP-Tokenizer`.

Kupietz, M., Lüngen, H., Kamocki, P., and Witt, A. (2018). The German reference corpus DeReKo: New developments – new opportunities. In *Proceedings of the 11th International Conference on Language Resources and Evaluation (LREC 2018), 7-12 May 2018, Miyazaki, Japan*, pages 4354–4360, Paris, France, May. European language resources association (ELRA).

Lesk, M. E. and Schmidt, E. (1975). Lex - A Lexical Analyzer Generator. Technical Report 39, Bell Laboratories, Murray Hill, NJ.

McDonald, R., Nivre, J., Quirmbach-Brundage, Y., Goldberg, Y., Das, D., Ganchev, K., Hall, K., Petrov, S., Zhang, H., Täckström, O., Bedini, C., Bertomeu Castelló, N., and Lee, J. (2013). Universal Dependency Annotation for Multilingual Parsing. In *Proceedings of the 51st Annual Meeting of the Association for Computational Linguistics (Volume 2: Short Papers)*, pages 92–97, Sofia, Bulgaria, August. Association for Computational Linguistics.

Mizobuchi, S., Sumitomo, T., Fuketa, M., and Aoe, J.-i. (2000). An efficient representation for implementing finite state machines based on the double-array. *Information Sciences*, 129(1):119–139, November.

Niu, S., Liu, Y., and Song, X. (2013). Speeding Up Double-Array Trie Construction for String Matching. In Yuyu Yuan, et al., editors, *Trustworthy Computing and Services*, Communications in Computer and Information Science, pages 572–579, Berlin, Heidelberg. Springer.

Ortmann, K., Roussel, A., and Dipper, S. (2019). Evaluating off-the-shelf NLP tools for german. In *Proceedings of the 15th Conference on Natural Language Processing (KONVENS 2019): Long Papers*, pages 212–222, Erlangen, Germany. German Society for Computational Linguistics & Language Technology.

Proisl, T. and Uhrig, P. (2016). SoMaJo: State-of-the-art tokenization for German web and social media texts. In *Proceedings of the 10th Web as Corpus Workshop*, pages 57–62, Berlin, August. Association for Computational Linguistics.

Song, X., Salcianu, A., Song, Y., Dopson, D., and Zhou, D. (2021). Fast WordPiece Tokenization. In *Proceedings of the 2021 Conference on Empirical Methods in Natural Language Processing*, pages 2089–2103, Online and Punta Cana, Dominican Republic, November. Association for Computational Linguistics.

Count-Based and Predictive Language Models for Exploring DeReKo

Peter Fankhauser, Marc Kupietz
Leibniz Institute for the German Language
Mannheim, Germany
{fankhauser|kupietz}@ids-mannheim.de

Abstract

We present the use of count-based and predictive language models for exploring language use in the German Reference Corpus DeReKo. For collocation analysis along the syntagmatic axis we employ traditional association measures based on co-occurrence counts as well as predictive association measures derived from the output weights of skipgram word embeddings. For inspecting the semantic neighbourhood of words along the paradigmatic axis we visualize the high dimensional word embeddings in two dimensions using t-stochastic neighbourhood embeddings. Together, these visualizations provide a complementary, explorative approach to analysing very large corpora in addition to corpus querying. Moreover, we discuss count-based and predictive models w.r.t. scalability and maintainability in very large corpora.

Keywords: language models, word embeddings, collocation analysis

1. Introduction

Distributional semantics is concerned with analysing language use based on the distributional properties of words derived from large corpora. In this paper we describe DeReKoVecs[1] (Fankhauser and Kupietz, 2017), a visualization of distributional word properties derived from the German Reference Corpus DeReKo[2] (Kupietz et al., 2010) comprising more than 53 billion tokens of written contemporary German.

DeReKoVecs represents the syntagmatic context of words in a window of five words to the left and to the right $w_{-5} \dots w_{-1}\, w\, w_1 \dots w_5$ as vectors. These vectors are either count-based or predictive.

The count-based models are computed by various association measures based on (co-occurrence) frequencies in the corpus; for an overview see e.g. Evert (2008).

The predictive models are trained using structured skipgrams (Ling et al., 2015), an extension of word2vec (Mikolov et al., 2013) that represents the individual positions in the syntagmatic context of a word separately, rather than lumping them together into a bag of words. Figures 1 and 2 compare count-based and predictive models for a word w in its left/right syntagmatic context with collocates $w_{-2}\, w_{-1}\, \_\, w_1\, w_2$.

The count-based model represents each pair $w_i\, w$ individually by some association measure o_i. With a vocabulary size of v (the number of different words, aka types) this leads to a very high dimensional model with order $O(v^2)$ parameters, where each word is represented by a sparse vector of size $4 * v$.

In contrast, the predictive model introduces a hidden layer h of size d. d is typically in the range of 50 to 300 and thus much smaller than v, which in the case of DeReKo ranges in the millions. Each word can thereby be represented by a much smaller vector of size d, also called its word embedding. Importantly, estimates of the association strength between w and its left and right collocates can still be gained via its output activations[3].

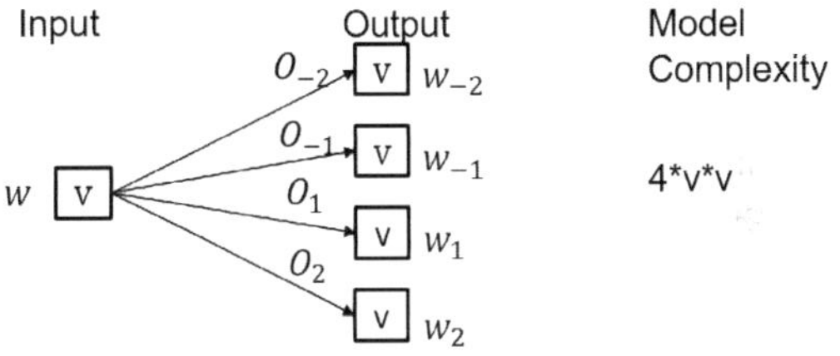

Figure 1: Count-based Model

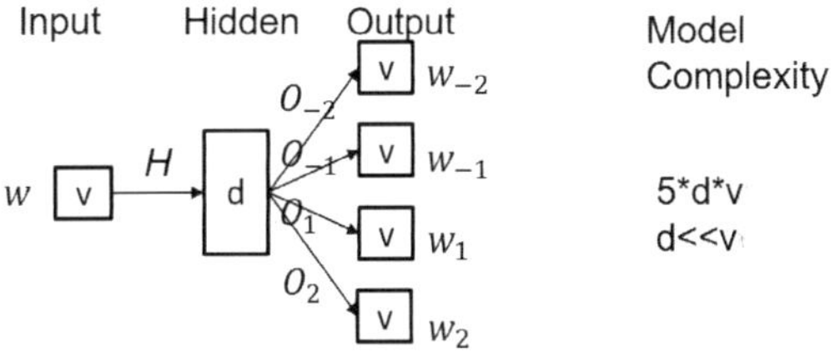

Figure 2: Predictive Model

Both models support the analysis of word use along the paradigmatic and the syntagmatic axis. Paradigmatically related words, such as synonyms or (co-)hyponyms, which occur in similar syntagmatic contexts, can be identified by determining the similarity (usually cosine similarity) between their vectors, which are, by construc-

[1] http://corpora.ids-mannheim.de/openlab/derekovecs

[2] https://www1.ids-mannheim.de/kl/projekte/korpora/

[3] More specifically, the output activations approximate the shifted pointwise mutual information. $SPMI(w, w_i) = log(\frac{p(w,w_i)}{p(w)p(w_i)}) - log(k)$, with k the number of negative samples used during training (see Levy and Goldberg 2014). Pointwise mutual information is one of the count-based collocation measures in DeReKoVecs.

Proceedings of the CMLC-10 Workshop (@LREC 2022), pages 27–31
Marseille, 20 June 2022

Kuh	German	English
Count	Kalles **heilige blöde Blinde Bunte** lila Rosmarie **dumme** Yvonne **Eis**	Kalle's **holy silly blind colorful** purple Rosemary **stupid** Yvonne **ice**
Pred	ausgebüxte geschlachtete entlaufene geklonte trächtige geschlachteten weidende verwesende Kalles tote	escaped slaughtered runaway cloned pregnant slaughtered grazing decaying Kalle's dead

Table 1: Count-based and predictive collocates for 'Kuh' ('cow')

tion, a representation of their syntagmatic contexts. Syntagmatically related words, which occur close to each other more often than expected, are represented by their count-based or computed association strength.
Count-based models and predictive models complement each other. Count-based models excel at representing all actually occurring, possibly polysemous usages, but they just memorize and do not generalize to other possible usages. In particular, they can fail to adequately represent low frequency words and collocations for which there simply do not exist enough examples. Predictive models generalize by means of dimensionality reduction in the hidden layer and thus can also predict unseen but meaningful usages, but they typically only represent the dominant, usually literal usage [4].
In the following we illustrate the interplay between count-based and predictive models along the syntagmatic and the paradigmatic axis by way of example.

2. Syntagmatic Analysis

Tables 1, 2 and 3 exemplify the interplay between count-based and predictive collocations[5].
Among the top 10 count-based collocates of 'Kuh' (cow), there are 6 collocates (in bold) stemming from idiomatic use, for example, 'die Kuh vom Eis kriegen' literally for 'getting the cow from the ice' meaning 'working out a situation'. In contrast, the predictive collocates all pertain to the literal meaning of cow as a (domestic) animal; e.g., 'Eis' does not occur among the top 400 predictive collocates.

[4]This focus on the dominant usage may be one of the main reasons for the relative success of predictive models as opposed to count-based models for lexical semantics tasks observed in (Baroni et al., 2014), as these tasks tend to focus on dominant semantics.

[5]We employ a variety of measures for the association strength between collocates. Here we only use the default measures: LogDice for count-based and the sum of output weights for the given word w normalized by the total weights for all words w_i. Both are restricted to those words w_i which maximize the measure.

Versuch	German	English
Count	unternommen gescheitert Beim zweiten gescheiterten wert dritten gestartet unternehmen scheiterte	made failed in second failed worth third started make failed
Pred	untauglicher vergeblicher missglückter unternommene krampfhaften fehlgeschlagener (...)	unsuitable futile failed made convulsive failed failed desperate unsuitable desperate

Table 2: Count-based and predictive collocates for 'Versuch' ('attempt')

Absatz	German	English
Count	**reißenden** Paragraf Paragraph **fanden** Berichtigung Satz Zeile **Reißenden** Grundgesetzes Aktualisierung	**soaring** paragraph **found** correction sentence line **soaring** constitution update
Pred	**reißenden reissenden rückläufigem** Unsinniger **Sinkender** bequellt **stagnierendem** unbelegten **reißend sinkendem**	**soaring declining** meaningless **decreasing** quoted/sourced **stagnant** unsubstantiated **soaring decreasing**

Table 3: Count-based and predictive collocates for 'Absatz' ('paragraph' vs. 'sales')

The count-based and predictive collocates of 'Versuch' ('attempt'), on the other hand, show no such difference. Both refer to the literal meaning of 'Versuch'. However, also here we can observe a bias of the predictive collocates towards a dominant usage as in 'failed attempts'.

Finally, the count-based and predictive collocates of 'Absatz' in Table 3 both comprise two usages/meanings: 'paragraph' and 'sales' (in bold). However, in particular the top count-based collocates for 'Absatz' as in 'sales' stem all from the fixed phrase 'reißenden Absatz finden' (literally: 'find soaring sales', roughly: 'sell like hotcakes'), whereas the predictive collocates cover a broader range of usages.

In summary, count-based collocates tend to come from fixed, possibly idiomatic phrases, whereas predictive collocates generalize to a broader range of words pertaining to a dominant meaning. An application of this discrepancy to detecting German idioms is described in Amin et al. (2021a; 2021b).

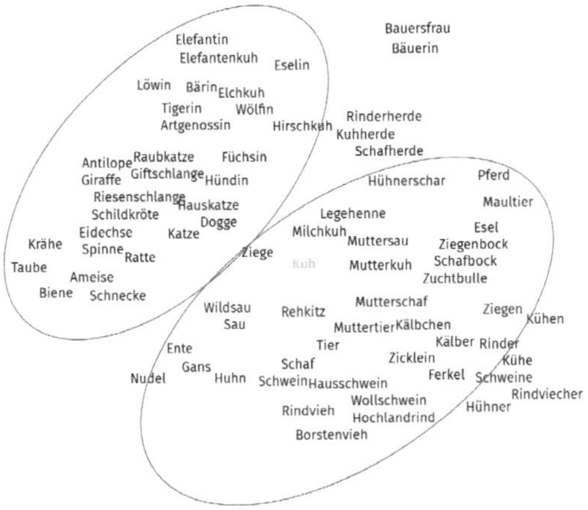

Figure 3: Paradigmatic neighbourhood of 'Kuh'

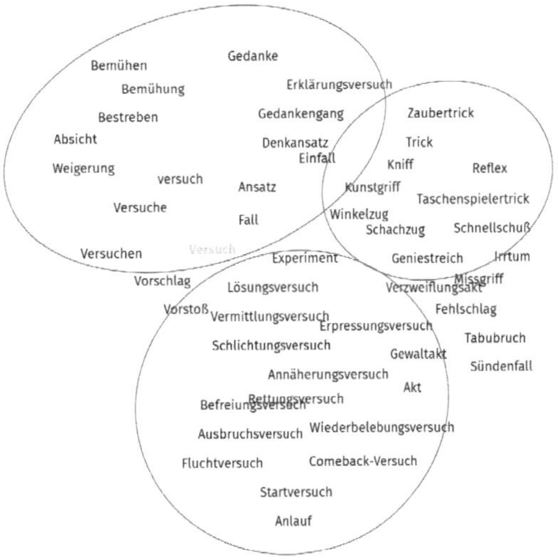

Figure 4: Paradigmatic neighbourhood of 'Versuch'

3. Paradigmatic Analysis

Looking at the paradigmatic axis for words with a similar usage context corroborates the syntagmatic analysis. Currently, we only provide for paradigmatic analysis on the basis of the predictive models but not based count-based models. For visualization we use t-stochastic neighbour embedding (t-sne, Van der Maaten and Hinton (2008)). T-sne maps the cosine distance between the high (200) dimensional word representations to two dimensions, such that small, local distances are preserved well, whereas global distances are not[6].

Figure 3 depicts the paradigmatic neighbourhood of 'Kuh' ('cow'). We can observe two main clusters, both referring to the literal meaning[7]. The top left cluster comprises wild animals, largely but not exclusively mammals, and the bottom right cluster comprises farm animals. The idiomatic use of 'Kuh' is not reflected[8].

The paradigmatic neighbourhood of 'Versuch' ('attempt', Figure 4) can be roughly divided into three clusters. 'Versuch' as a mental process (top left), 'Versuch' as a trick (top right), and as an action, usually expressed via a composite word (bottom).

Both 'Kuh' and 'Versuch' arguably only depict one broad meaning clustered into fine but nonetheless meaningful nuances. In contrast, the paradigmatic neighbourhood of 'Absatz' shown in Figure 5 gets clearly separated into 'paragraph' (left) and 'sales' (right). These two individual broad clusters can again be divided into fine grained subclusters (e.g. 'article', 'sentence', 'section' for 'paragraph'), but the big divide between 'paragraph' and 'sales' along the syntagmatic axis for both, the count-based and the predictive model, also shows along the paradigmatic axis.

4. Performance & Maintainability

An important motivation for us to experiment with word embedding models was the expectation that, thanks to efficient dimension reduction, they would be more performant to compute and more efficient to analyse in terms of paradigmatic neighbourhoods than the count-based models used so far in the context of the CCDB platform (Keibel and Belica, 2007).[9]

For the latter, the necessary precalculation of paradigmatic distances was considered to be so computationally expensive that it was hardly maintainable and the last calculation was carried out on the basis of DeReKo-2006-I, so that distributional analyses of the very current language use, based on DeReKo, was not possible for a long time.

We cannot yet draw a final conclusion regarding the performance comparisons, since we have not yet implemented paradigmatic analyses based on the count-based models. However, the computation time of the word embedding network for DeReKo-2022-I (53G tokens) is with 10 days roughly equivalent to the creation of a corresponding co-occurrence database,[10] each with 10 context words.[11] The disk space requirement is slightly larger with 61,2 GB vs. 45 GB in the case of the word embeddings.

As far as the runtime behaviour is concerned, it should be noted that for the calculation of the syntagmatic neighbours, the entire word embedding network is kept virtually in memory via memory mapping, so that if many

[6]Our visualization also provides for self organizing maps (SOM) (Kohonen, 1982), which position paradigmatic neighbourhoods on a grid of 6x6 squares.

[7]The ellipses are manually superimposed for the purpose of illustration.

[8]Incidently it is also not reflected in the count-based paradigmatic neighbourhood, not shown here.

[9]http://corpora.ids-mannheim.de/ccdb/

[10]based on RocksDB (Dong et al., 2021)

[11]on a Supermicro Intel(R) Xeon(R) Gold 6148 CPU Linux server with 80 cores @ 2.4 GHz and 756 GB RAM

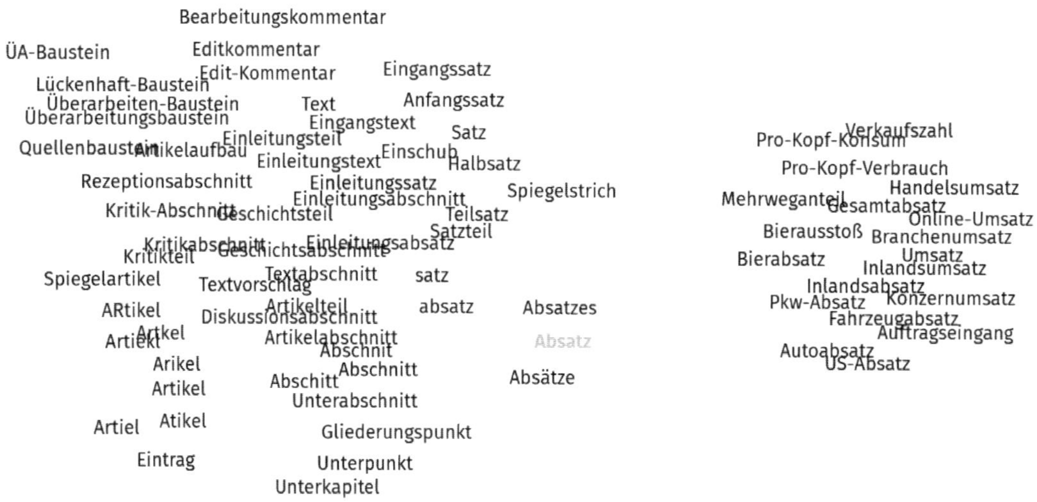

Figure 5: Paradigmatic neighbourhood of 'Absatz'

instances are required, the RAM requirement can become a bottleneck.

All in all, both the calculation and the runtime behaviour are in a range that allows an annual update and the continuous operation of up to five instances, in our case. The approach is also quite scalable. The calculation of the predictive models can be accelerated by using more processor cores and building the count-based model with faster disks. The integrity of the programmes is ensured by CI workflows with an increasing number of tests, maintainability by a small number of dependencies, and easy deployment by Dockerization. Only the extension is somewhat challenging, as the code is mainly written in C, C++ and Perl.[12]

5. Availability

All tools that have been used in this paper to compute and analyse the models and to visualize the results are published under the Apache License 2.0 and available open-source on our Gerrit code-review site.[13]

We are happy to share all count-based and predictive models with interested colleagues under the Text and Data Mining exception (§ 60d German Copyright Act) (see also Kamocki et al. 2018).

6. Conclusions

We have described the implementation and use of count-based and predictive models for syntagmatic and paradigmatic analysis of language use in the German Reference Corpus DeReKo. Currently, we work on two main lines of extending the presented approach: (1) To allow a more principled comparison between count-based and predictive association measures, we plan to map the output weights to actual co-occurrence predictions. (2) To be able to contrast language use in different contexts, such as register or time, we experiment with several approaches to train context-dependent word embeddings. Finally, we also plan to apply the presented approach to other corpora.

[12] see Diewald et al. (2021) for the relevance of such aspects for linguistic research (tools)

[13] https://korap.ids-mannheim.de/gerrit/plugins/gitiles/ids-kl/dereko2vec
https://korap.ids-mannheim.de/gerrit/plugins/gitiles/ids-kl/derekovecs

7. Acknowledgements

We thank our anonymous reviewers for helpful comments on earlier drafts of the manuscript.

8. Bibliographical References

Amin, M., Fankhauser, P., Kupietz, M., and Schneider, R. (2021a). Data-driven identification of idioms in song lyrics. In *Proceedings of the 17th Workshop on Multiword Expressions (MWE 2021)*, pages 13–22, Stroudsburg, PA. Association for Computational Linguistics.

Amin, M., Fankhauser, P., Kupietz, M., and Schneider, R. (2021b). Shallow context analysis for german idiom detection. In *Proceedings of the Shared Task on the Disambiguation of German Verbal Idioms at KONVENS 2021*.

Baroni, M., Dinu, G., and Kruszewski, G. (2014). Don't count, predict! a systematic comparison of context-counting vs. context-predicting semantic vectors. In *Proceedings of the 52nd Annual Meeting of the Association for Computational Linguistics (Volume 1: Long Papers)*, pages 238–247, Baltimore, Maryland, June. Association for Computational Linguistics.

Diewald, N., Margaretha, E., and Kupietz, M. (2021). Lessons learned in quality management for online research software tools in linguistics. In Harald Lüngen, et al., editors, *Proceedings of the Workshop on Challenges in the Management of Large Corpora (CMLC-9) 2021. Limerick, 12 July 2021 (Online-Event)*, pages 20 – 26, Mannheim. Leibniz-Institut für Deutsche Sprache.

Dong, S., Kryczka, A., Jin, Y., and Stumm, M. (2021). Rocksdb: Evolution of development priorities in a key-value store serving large-scale applications. *ACM Trans. Storage*, 17(4), oct.

Evert, S. (2008). Corpora and collocations. In Anke Lüdeling et al., editors, *Corpus Linguistics. An International Handbook*, chapter 58, pages 1212–1248. Mouton de Gruyter, Berlin, Germany.

Fankhauser, P. and Kupietz, M. (2017). Visualizing language change in a corpus of contemporary german. In *Corpus Linguistics Conference*, Birmingham, United Kingdom.

Kamocki, P., Ketzan, E., Wildgans, J., and Witt, A. (2018). New exceptions for Text and Data Mining and their possible impact on the CLARIN infrastructure. In Inguna Skadina et al., editors, *CLARIN Annual Conference 2018, Proceedings. 8-10 October 2018, Pisa, Italy*, pages 39 – 42, Utrecht. CLARIN.

Keibel, H. and Belica, C. (2007). CCDB: A corpus-linguistic research and development workbench. In *Proceedings of the 4th Corpus Linguistics Conference (CL 2007)*, Birmingham.

Kohonen, T. (1982). Self–organized formation of topologically correct feature maps. *Biological Cybernetics*, 43:59–69.

Kupietz, M., Belica, C., Keibel, H., and Witt, A. (2010). The German Reference Corpus DeReKo: A Primordial Sample for Linguistic Research. In Nicoletta Calzolari, et al., editors, *Proceedings of the Seventh conference on International Language Resources and Evaluation (LREC'10)*, pages 1848–1854, Valletta/Paris. European Language Resources Association (ELRA). http://www.lrec-conf.org/proceedings/lrec2010/pdf/414_Paper.pdf.

Levy, O. and Goldberg, Y. (2014). Neural word embedding as implicit matrix factorization. In *Advances in Neural Information Processing Systems (NIPS)*.

Ling, W., Dyer, C., Black, A. W., and Trancoso, I. (2015). Two/too simple adaptations of Word2Vec for syntax problems. In *Proceedings of the 2015 Conference of the North American Chapter of the Association for Computational Linguistics: Human Language Technologies*, pages 1299–1304, Denver, Colorado, May–June. Association for Computational Linguistics.

Mikolov, T., Sutskever, I., Chen, K., Corrado, G. S., and Dean, J. (2013). Distributed representations of words and phrases and their compositionality. In C. J. C. Burges, et al., editors, *Advances in Neural Information Processing Systems*, volume 26. Curran Associates, Inc.

Van der Maaten, L. and Hinton, G. E. (2008). Visualizing data using t-sne. *Journal of Machine Learning Research*, 9:2579–2605, November.

"The word expired when that world awoke." New Challenges for Research with Large Text Corpora and Corpus-Based Discourse Studies in Totalitarian Times.

Hanno Biber
Austrian Academy of Sciences
Bäckerstraße 13, 1010 Vienna
Hanno.Biber@oeaw.ac.at

Abstract

The title's opening quotation is a translation of the final line of the famous poem by the satirist Karl Kraus from 1933 that explains in ten lines the limits of language use when violence reigns, something that can be seen as a fundamental research question. The prospects of a possible corpus project based upon the AAC-Austrian Academy Corpus, established in 2001, will be assessed to give answers to questions concerning the research challenges for large digital text corpora in the context of studying totalitarian language. The AAC contains many German language texts from the first half on the 20th century and can be regarded as a valuable diachronic corpus suitable for corpus-based studies focused upon historical sources. Therefore it might be used not only to document the language of the time of the rise of the Nazis in Germany and Austria, but may also lead to giving an example as to how apply such an approach to related issues of addressing the challenges of critically using contemporary text corpora in the context of a new totalitarianism unfolding by the Russian war of extermination in Ukraine and its lexical representations in the discourses of contemporary media full of propaganda and disinformation.

Keywords: propaganda, critical discourse studies, corpus linguistics

1. Research Challenges

In the following paper, first, a report on and a description of the prospects of a corpus project will be given that could possibly be initiated by one of the large historical diachronic digital text corpora hosted by the Austrian Academy of Sciences, the AAC – Austrian Academy Corpus. And second, new potential challenges for corpus linguistic research with large contemporary synchronic digital text corpora will be addressed with a particular reference to lexical representations to be found in text corpora with regard to discourse phenomena to be observed in contemporary media and current news in particular. Furthermore, these challenges for large text corpora will be viewed focusing on phenomena to be observed in digital media that are to a very large extent full of propaganda and disinformation, above all in times that can not only hyperbolically but also have with sound historical reason to be viewed as evolving into new totalitarian times now. On this occasion, however only a rather fine outline for such an extensive framework for corpus research can be made, so that the rough idea presented should rather be regarded as a research proposal and as a suggestion for future projects. First, the digital resources of the AAC – Austrian Academy Corpus, that has been founded in 2001 (cf. Biber and Breiteneder, 2002), which is one of the very valuable examples of considerably large diachronic digital text corpora also suitable for corpus-based discourse studies and for digital corpus-based lexicography grounded upon historical text sources, can be used as a starting point for trying to answer new questions concerning the challenges for doing linguistic research with large digital text corpora in the context of studying totalitarian language use. The questions, as well as the chances and the limits of such an approach, have very obvious actual references to the historic events unfolding today as well as a clearly historical dimension, precisely because the digital text sources that have been created to analyze the German language use of the Nazi-period from 1933 to 1945 can be understood as a model to deal with related questions of contemporary language use, particularly in the context of the new Russian war of extermination in Ukraine of today and particularly how it is represented in contemporary media. It stands to reason that corpus linguistics and historical language studies are not performed in a sphere free from ideological, social, political, nationalistic, and related implications. The dynamics of an increasing influence of information in data-driven societies with industrialized and algorithmically enhanced linguistic activities in the field of political propaganda demands from researchers to be quickly able to address these questions in order to contribute to an enlightened and scientifically tenable perspective on the observed processes, for which large text corpora have already been built and for corpora which are urgently needed to be constructed for such purposes. Linguistic content challenges are particularly prevalent when confronted with various phenomena that are to be observed in historical sources just like in contemporary sources, such as "atrocity propaganda", "industrialized lies", "fear discourse", "alternative facts", "obfuscation techniques", "information warfare" and similar events that are to be detected in large quantities of digital content created, be it in form of diachronic text corpora or in synchronic corpora.

2. Diachronic Text

2.1 AAC – Austrian Academy Corpus

The AAC – Austrian Academy Corpus was founded in 2001 and has been created as a corpus linguistic research project undertaken within the framework of the Austrian Academy of Sciences in Vienna in the first decade of the 21st century. The AAC is a German language text corpus of more than fivehundredmillion tokens and represents a large diachronic digital text corpus with several thousands of German language texts of important historical and cultural significance. The AAC-Austrian Academy Corpus has an emphasis also on literary and political journals as well as

Proceedings of the CMLC-10 Workshop (@LREC 2022), pages 32–35
Marseille, 20 June 2022

on collections of texts that are difficult to obtain in or difficult to integrate into digital text resources. Overall, the texts of the AAC are predominantly German language texts from the period between 1848 and 1989, ranging from the 1848 revolution to the fall of the iron curtain in 1989, but have a focus on the first half of the twentieth century. "The time frame and the text frame of these highly valuable digital collections of German language texts from all over the German speaking areas constitute the first two important dimensions of the text corpus and its research approaches which are based upon a variety of different parameters." (Biber, 2020) These parameters are also of empirical and historical as well as of dimensions of linguistic domains. Among the sources of the AAC a very large number of texts of the historical period in question in this report have been collected, digitized, converted into machine-readable text and annotated and been provided with metadata, according to the standards of structural and thematic mark-up applied then, of annotation and mark-up schemes based upon XML almost two decades ago. In a presentation of this project an overview of the necessary methodological considerations and an outline of the research perspectives based upon the principles of corpus linguistics should be given, but as this has been done in several previous presentations, the references to the respective publications should suffice (cf. Biber and Breiteneder, 2002; Biber, 2004; Biber and Breiteneder, 2004; Biber and Breiteneder, 2012; Biber and Breiteneder, 2014).

2.2 Subcorpus of 1933-1945

The topic of the proposed research project to be paid attention here, is focused on the questions of developing a diachronic text corpus of historical significance and establishing a corpus based research environment for language studies of the historical period between 1933 and 1945, with particular emphasis on the year 1933, the year when the Nazis came to power in Germany. As the core of the AAC is from the first half of the twentieth century, the research issue of an analysis of the German language of the time between 1933 and 1945 is feasible and can be done comprehensively. Corpus-based approaches for analyzing the language exploring the historical periods before, during and after Nazi rule together have been rare, despite numerous more detailed scholarly works in the fields of historical studies as well as in German language studies. (cf. Biber, 2010) Building a diachronic digital text corpus for historical German language studies of this particular kind is a challenging task for various reasons. There are certain technical difficulties of corpus building in dealing with a large historical variety of different genres and text types, and the "specific historical parameters and the methodological scope of such an investigation" (Biber and Breiteneder, 2013) have to be taken into consideration. The German language of the years between 1933 and 1945 is being considered as a historical focal point for which an exemplary corpus-based research methodology for the study of the German language can be developed. "The sources of a first exemplary study will cover manifold domains and genres, not only newspapers and political journals and magazines, which will be at the core, but also several other text types representing the historical communicative strategies" can be integrated in such a research initiative. (Biber and Breiteneder, 2013) Among the text sources to be considered, are not only political speeches, pamphlets, flyers, or advertisements, but also essays and literary texts as well as possibly radio programs, or even administrative, scientific and legal texts, which have been already collected to some extent (cf. Biber and Breiteneder, 2013). In this case not primarily the well-known documents and the evident language of the Nazi period could be included in the analysis, but systematically less easily visible documents and less significant lexical items might also be taken into consideration. This methodological approach is considered as particularly promising by means of applying methods of corpus linguistics and by testing new strategies of the application of these methods in the context of historical language studies. The AAC corpus holdings may provide a large number of interesting resources and lead to corpus-based approaches for investigations into the texts of the historical period in question. (cf. Biber and Breiteneder, 2013) "Quantitative corpus linguistics has proofed to be a valuable technique in many domains of philological, sociological and historical research. The digitized and linguistically annotated corpus is therefore an interesting source for studies in many fields and facilitates the investigation of changing patterns of language use, and how these reflect underlying cultural shifts." (Volk, 2010). And one may ask, if a practical combination of corpus linguistics, lexicography, historical studies, discourse analysis and cultural studies can be used to gain knowledge about the texts of the time in focus.

2.3 1933 and the Following

"The word expired when that world awoke", is the quotation in the title of this paper and a translation by Max Knight (Zohn, 1990) of the last line of the famous poem by the satirist Karl Kraus written in September 1933 and originally published in his satirical journal in the issue of October 1933 (Biber, 2007). Its interpretation is used in order to refer to a crucial challenge for all linguistic research and language studies, to be deliberately formulated here, as indicated, as a particular challenge for corpus research in a particular historical context. Answers to the questions posed with regard to analyzing the language of a certain historical period might be found in analytically making use of the long analytical text written by Karl Kraus between May and September 1993, which has not been published in his journal and for which the poem however functioned as an indicator and index. This long unpublished text from 1933, that was only posthumously published in 1952 for the first time, bears the title "The Third Walpurgis Night" and has only very recently been translated into English. (Kraus, 2021) With the help of this text, that opens up a critical analytical path for language research, exploring the large digital text corpus of German language texts from the first half of the twentieth century, could be achieved in a confident manner. At the Austrian Academy of Sciences a new digital German text edition has been published, for which a register of the many texts and documents quoted and a "register of personal names" (Biber, 2021) has been created of more than 400 perpetrators, victims and witnesses appearing in the text, where the crimes and the language of the time of the rise of the Nazis in Germany and in Austria are documented. The text could function as an example as to how to deal with documents in the context of the mentioned challenges for large text corpora in totalitarian times. "The Third Walpurgis Night" is the most important text and a most detailed contemporary account of German literature about the horrifying origins and deadly consequences of National-Socialism, where the murderous reality and the murderous language of the Nazis is documented in many examples as early as May 1933, examples that are quoted and then commented upon, with insights which can be taken as starting points for conducting the proposed research within the frameworks of a large text corpus. “As to Hitler I have nothing to say” is the famous first sentence of this long text that, significantly, concludes after more than 300 pages of analyzing Nazi language and Nazi atrocities with a quotation from Goethe’s Faust II, that “may this phantom”, the tyrant and his regime, be “hurled among the dead”, a sentence said as in the face of total violence the word is inappropriate. (Kraus, 2020) The author decided not to publish his text, but to conserve it for posterity and the text dealing with the language and the violence as well as the consequences of their political developments for the world is just very briefly summarized in the final line of his poem, as quoted above. The AAC – Austrian Academy Corpus contains very many documents from the time and many documents that are also dealt with in the text of 1933, with texts and of “what appeared, day by day, in print, on the radio, and in public forums.” (Perloff, 2020). Significant parts are not only dealing with the “rhetoric of respected thinkers” (Perloff, 2020) who were advocating and agitating in favour of Nazism, like the philosopher and university rector Martin Heidegger, or the poet and medical doctor Gottfried Benn, but also treating the former philologist and journalist Goebbels, the Nazi Minister of Propaganda and his language technique, which is more than interesting in this case, where an account and a linguistic discourse analysis of a Reichstag speech is given, where Goebbels “has attitude and empathy, he knows about the stimulus and impetus, application and implication, dramatic presentation, filmic transposition, flexible formulation, and the other aides to radical renewal, he has experience and perspective, indeed for both reality and vision, he has zest for life and world-philosophy, he approves of ethos and pathos but also mythos, he supplies subordination and integration into the living-space and working space of the nation, he embraces the emotional realm of community and the vitalism of personality.” (Kraus, 2020) The language of totalitarianism is to be clearly observed in the year in which the Nazis came to power in Germany and because of the analysis by Karl Kraus no one can deny the fact that it had been possible then to predict where this would lead to, to annihilation and finally to extermination.

3. Synchronic Text

3.1 Context of Contemporary Corpora

Digital text corpora of today are to an increasing extent more and more based upon sources from contemporary news cycles, newspapers, media outlets, social media content etc. The communicative frame in which linguistic expression and language is set, becomes more and more important. Contemporary language production, that to a very large extent is of journalistic origin and can possibly function as sources for linguistic research by means of large text corpora, needs to be studied and analysed in detail. This is of particular importance in times when the mechanisms of war-driven communication and the discursive distortions and manipulations of totalitarian propaganda is becoming to be dominant in public discourse. A critical viewpoint is more than necessary in order to successfully analyse also text corpus content yet to be substantially formed into useable text corpora out of the vast amount of contemporary news and discourse cycles. And it is equally important to critically understand and do substantial research about the propaganda propagating in the media of today, let alone those which are openly and aggressively neglecting, ignoring, obfuscating, distorting the atrocities committed in a criminal war. It is obvious that this happens in a principally problematic situation of journalism that has been described even for the times before the First World War or shortly after by the language and media critic. The “rogue profession” that “takes the audience for an idiot” to “outwit their intelligence with its own mindlessness” and “abuses the debility which is called public opinion for any infamy” (Biber 2007), as Karl Kraus describes in still democratic June 1923 the relation of the public and journalism together with politics, demonstrates that journalism in all its forms is the main object of critique, in texts whose conclusions have still validity for old and new media systems alike, as even Jonathan Franzen as translator and commentator has observed in his book “The Kraus Project”. (Franzen, 2013) Karl Kraus has blamed and named the “pyramidal dimensions of stupidity” as “the secret of all journalistic seduction”, in which the dispositions of the journalistic audience and the journalistic profession meet, and who, in the cited article in his journal, has pointed at “the stolen pathos of the just cause, which no other rogue profession has so easily at hand as this one, that as a means for exploitation always takes the audience for an idiot in order to outwit their intelligence with its own mindlessness and abuses the debility which is called public opinion for any infamy, while the impotence which is called the state authority has become an inactive witness.” (Biber, 2007). The satirist views the audience not only as a victim of journalistic practice, but also as an accomplice in the journalistic crime of stupidity and absurdity. The very notion of public opinion is already an absurdity and a logic contradiction for him, who reminds his own audience of the necessary private nature of any opinion and demands not only sincerity from the sender but also a sincere subjectivity and critical awareness from the receiver of a news message, so that an opinion can be formed by the audience and is not at all preformed and engineered by the opinion business beforehand. This complex is to be taken seriously in the context of doing corpus linguistic research with journalistic texts, where the researcher is much more than just another audience of the language production but more of a critical analyst of what can be observed.

3.2 2022 and the Following

Corpus linguistics and literary studies in the 21st century must be working and doing research in the context of a technologically and ideologically dynamic historical situation and therefore be aware of the difficulties and necessities for the research. The computer technologies and their algorithmic potential, the impacts of social media, digital archives, digital libraries, and many other phenomena of the contemporary world of technological communication and information technology demonstrate how much the ways of thinking, speaking, writing, and communicating are determined by technical acceleration. What it means to read, understand and examine with scientific means the texts in a digitalized world and how the sources of information must be investigated with new tools in this context of new modes of communication and new forms of text production, also demand new methods for corpus linguistics and language research. For this purpose it is necessary to construct and create an infrastructure of suitable text corpora enabling the researchers to study the described phenomena with the help of corpus linguistic methodologies. The research focus must be determined by well-established methods in combination with a critical apparatus based upon insights of media critique and therefore enable the researchers to find, determine and select as well as carefully analyze the texts in digital corpora. This process of integrating and aggregating texts form various resources should lead to the creation of a new research environment for corpus linguists useful also for synchronic purposes. The German language use of aggression during the Nazi-period and the critical analysis based upon Krausian critique of language use can function as a model to deal with contemporary questions of violent language use, above all in the example of the setting of today's Russian war of extermination in Ukraine. The ways in which and the role how digital and conventional media texts and their linguistic inventories play a role in this war and are used by the aggressor, and how the aggression has been prepared for years by propagandistic interventions in contemporary media, certainly needs to be investigated by means of corpus linguistics as well. Corpus linguistics and historical language studies are not done without ideological, social, political, nationalistic, and other related implications. The dynamics of information warfare in connection with industrialized and algorithmically enhanced linguistic activities in the field of political propaganda demands from researchers to be quickly able to address the issues of coming to terms with language production and linguistic elements that can be followed scientifically by means of corpus linguistics. One has to be aware of the diabolic (obviously Mephistophelian) fact that historical progress is always moving on and that, even when it seems to be over, history will repeat itself and the past will become the future, as the eighth and ninth lines of the quoted poem reminds one: "It cannot last; Later it all was past." (Bridgham and Timms, 2020)" Or as the same lines read in the other translation: "Time marches on; the final difference is none." (cf. Zohn, 1990) New large text corpora need to be built and these text corpora are urgently needed to be constructed for purposes of analyzing texts in the described contexts. The challenges just very briefly explained here are particularly demanding when in contemporary sources discourse phenomena of "atrocity propaganda", "industrialized lies", "fear discourse", "alternative facts", "obfuscation techniques", "information warfare" etc. are to be observed in journalistic texts, all occurrences to be detected in large quantities in large text corpora, diachronic or synchronic.

4. Bibliographical References

Biber, H. and Breiteneder, E. (2002): Austrian Academy Corpus: digital resources in textual studies. In: J. Anderson, A. Dunning, M. Fraser (eds.): *Digital Resources for the Humanities 2001–2002. An edited selection of papers.* (Publication 16) London: Office for Humanities Communication, p. 13-18

Biber, H. and Breiteneder, E. (2004): "The AAC [Austrian Academy Corpus] - An Enterprise to Develop Large Electronic Text Corpora". In: M. L. Lino, M. F. Xavier et al. (Eds.): *Proceedings of the 4th International Conference on Language Resources and Evaluation Lisbon 2004. Volume V*, Lisbon: ELRA, p. 1803-1806

Biber, H. et al. (Eds.) (2007): AAC-Austrian Academy Corpus 2007: AAC-Fackel. Online Version: "Die Fackel. Herausgeber: Karl Kraus, Wien 1899-1936". AAC Digital Edition No 1, fackel.oeaw.ac.at

Biber, H. (2010): "Aufbruch der Phrase zur Tat". Kommunikationsmaßnahmen und sprachliche Formungen der nationalsozialistischen Machtübernahme in Österreich 1938. In: Welzig. W et al. (Eds.) (2010): *Anschluss. März/April 1938 in Österreich.* Vienna: Austrian Academy of Sciences Press, p. 15-37

Biber, H. and Breiteneder, E. (2012): Fivehundredmillionandone Tokens. Loading the AAC Container with Text Resources for Text Studies. In: N. Calzolari et al. (Eds.): *Proceedings of the International Conference on Language Resources and Evaluation LREC 2012, Istanbul, 23.-25. 5. 2012.* Istanbul: ELRA, p. 1067-1070

Biber, H. and Breiteneder, E. (2013): The German Language of the Year 1933. Building a Diachronic Text Corpus for Historical German Language Studies. In: Center for Digital Research in the Humanities (Ed.): *Digital Humanities 2013 Proceedings.* Lincoln: University of Nebraska, p. 107-109

H. Biber and E. Breiteneder (2014): Text Corpora for Text Studies. About the foundations of the AAC - Austrian Academy Corpus. In: H. Biber, et. al (eds.) (2014): *Challenges in the management of large corpora (CMLC-2) LREC 2014 Workshop-Proceedings.* Reykjavik: LREC, p. 30-34

Biber, H. (2020): Challenges for Making Use of a Large Text Corpus such as the 'AAC – Austrian Academy Corpus' for Digital Literary Studies. In: Banski, P., et al. (Eds.) (2020): *LREC 2020 Workshop. 8th Workshop on Challenges in the Management of Large Corpora (CMLC-8), Proceedings.* Marseille: ELRA, p. 47-51

Biber, H. (2021): Personenregister. Karl Kraus 1933: Dritte Walpurgisnacht. kraus1933.ace.oeaw.ac.at

Bridgham, F. and Timms, E. (2020): Introduction. In: Kraus, K. (2020): *The Third Walpurgis Night.* New Haven: Yale University Press, p. xix-xxv

Franzen, J. (2013): The Kraus Project: Essays by Karl Kraus. New York: MacMillan

Kraus, K. (2020): The Third Walpurgis Night. [The Complete Text Translated from the German by Fred Bridgham and Edward Timms]. New Haven: Yale University Press

Perloff, M. (2020): Foreword. In: Kraus, K. (2020): *The Third Walpurgis Night.* New Haven: Yale University Press, p. vii-xv

Volk, M. et al. (2010): Challenges in building a multilingual alpine heritage corpus. In: N. Calzolari et al. (Eds.): *Proceedings of the International Conference on Language Resources and Evaluation LREC 2012, Istanbul, 23.-25. 5. 2012.* Istanbul: ELRA, p. 1653-1659

Zohn, H. (1990) (Ed.). Karl Kraus - In These Great Times. Chicago: University Press

5. Language Resource References

AAC - Austrian Academy Corpus (2001)

Author Index